evolutionary thought in psychology:
A Brief History

Blackwell Brief Histories of Psychology

The *Blackwell Brief Histories of Psychology* offer concise, accessible, and lively accounts of key topics within psychology, such as emotion, intelligence, and stress, that have had a profound effect on psychological and cultural life. The books in this series provide a rich sense of historical context while remaining grounded in contemporary issues and research that will be of interest to both academic and general readers.

Stress: A Brief History
Cary L. Cooper and Philip Dewe

Evolutionary Thought in Psychology: A Brief History
Henry Plotkin

Emotions: A Brief History
Keith Oatley

Intelligence: A Brief History
Anna T. Cianciolo and Robert J. Sternberg

evolutionary thought in psychology

A Brief History

HENRY PLOTKIN

Blackwell
Publishing

© 2004 by Henry Plotkin

350 Main Street, Malden, MA 02148-5020, USA
108 Cowley Road, Oxford OX4 1JF, UK
550 Swanston Street, Carlton, Victoria 3053, Australia

The right of Henry Plotkin to be identified as the Author of this
Work has been asserted in accordance with the UK Copyright,
Designs, and Patents Act 1988.

First published 2004 by Blackwell Publishing Ltd

Library of Congress Cataloging-in-Publication Data

Plotkin, H. C. (Henry C.)
Evolutionary thought in psychology : a brief history / Henry Plotkin.
p. cm. — (Blackwell brief histories of psychology ; 2)
Includes bibliographical references (p.   ) and index.
ISBN 1-4051-1377-4 (hbk : alk. paper) — ISBN 1-4051-1378-2
(pbk : alk. paper)
1. Evolutionary psychology—History. I. Title. II. Series.

BF698.95.P575 2004
155.7—dc22

2003028027

A catalogue record for this title is available from the British Library.

Set in 10/12pt Book Antique
by Kolam Information Services Pvt. Ltd, Pondicherry, India
Printed and bound in the United Kingdom
by TJ International, Padstow, Cornwall

For further information on
Blackwell Publishing, visit our website:
http://www.blackwellpublishing.com

In memory of my parents

Contents

Preface

Charles Darwin knew that extending the theory of evolution to a science of the human mind was an exercise of supreme importance. It took decades for this to be done with any kind of conceptual competence, and about a century was to pass before psychology itself came to understand that a science of mind without an evolutionary perspective is incomplete. This is a history of those early fumbled attempts, the banishment of evolution along with virtually all theory by the shameful rise and reign over significant swathes of psychology of behaviorism and its accompanying hard-line empiricist stance with regard to the assumed unbounded nature of human faculties, the inevitable rise of evolutionary thinking in the study of animal behavior, and its final incorporation within a defensible framework into a science of the human mind itself.

Whilst the book traces the history of the slow struggle to achieve Darwin's ambition, two things must be made clear at the outset to the reader. This book is **not** a history of the evolutionary psychology of the last twenty years or so, and nor is it a survey of contemporary evolutionary psychology. The systematic analysis of psychological process and mechanism from an evolutionary perspective, and its accompanying empirical program, is very recent—too recent for an historical account. It is simply impossible to know with certainty what will prove to be the important and enduring concepts and findings and what are the trivial, if sensational. In exactly the same way as it would have been impossible in the period around 1880–90 to have predicted how either evolutionary biology or psychology as individual sciences would develop over the decades to follow on the basis of work and thought of the previous twenty years when both were born as new sciences, so it is not possible to pronounce beyond an informed guess as to what kinds of evolutionary ideas and what forms of empirical studies will be dominating in 2020 as a result of how evolutionary psychology looks today. What is certain is that evolutionary thinking in psychology is here to stay and will prove significant, but precisely how is not the concern of this book. So what is presented in the following pages is a broad history of evolutionary thought within psychology, and not a detailed history of evolutionary psychology itself as it has appeared over the last two decades. It should also be noted that neither is this a history of psychology, and so what would be serious omissions in a general history, for instance the Gestalt school or psychometrics, have no relevance here since they had no bearing on the incorporation of evolutionary thinking into the discipline.

As will be seen, I use a principle of specific application of evolution to issues in the science of mind as the unifying theme that gives a coherence to this history. It is in the light of that principle, in combination with what were the clear initial studies in the birth of contemporary evolutionary psychology, on which chapter 7 is built. This book in general, and chapter 7 in particular, is not a comprehensive survey of contemporary evolutionary psychology. There are a dozen and more books competing in that role at present, and this is not one of those.

Academic writing is too often its own worst enemy. The detailed naming of names with accompanying dates is avoided within the main text. A brief listing of relevant references on a chapter by chapter basis is given at the end of the book, and I have tried where possible to keep those references friendly and available rather than forbidding tracts buried in obscure journals. If there is any single scholarly work that people should go to if my humble efforts succeed in arousing interest, it is to Robert J. Richards' magnificent *Darwin and the Emergence of Evolutionary Theories of Mind and Behavior*.

My thanks to Phyllis Wentworth who first interested me in the idea of writing this brief history. I am also grateful for the guidance of Christine Cardone of Blackwell. Gillian Brown, Robin Dunbar, Celia Heyes, David Hull, Kevin Laland, and George Mandler read one or more chapters. Phyllis Wentworth read the entire manuscript. I am indebted to them for their generosity and kindness in doing so, and for their comments and corrections. Any errors, waywardness, or serious omissions, are, of course, to be laid at my door and not theirs.

London
September 2003

CHAPTER ONE

Curious Histories

The Greek geographer and astronomer Ptolemy proposed around 150 A.D. that the Earth is the center of the universe. Based on the notion that a circle is a perfect form, together with what was then known about astronomical cycles, the Ptolemaic model conceived of the moon, the sun, the planets apart from the Earth, and all of the stars, as being in circular orbits around our planet. This view held for almost one-and-a-half thousand years. But as astronomical observation improved and accumulated the idea of circles within circles with the Earth at the center began to seem less certain. Nicolaus Copernicus, polymathic Polish adviser to governments and Popes, had pondered upon the Ptolemaic conception for decades whilst contemplating reform of the calendar. Copernicus was bothered both by the complexity of Ptolemy's scheme and the seeming inaccuracies of astronomical observation when mapped onto the Ptolemaic model. One possible solution to the failure of the observations to match the model well was to consider the model wrong, and Copernicus began to conjecture about the possibility that the Sun, not the Earth, was the center of all things. He developed a simple scheme, still based on circular orbits (Kepler later corrected this with elliptical orbits), which seemed to fit better with the astronomical data. Such data, however, were observations made with the naked eye and difficult to quantify with any accuracy. Copernicus knew that in offering an alternative model to that of Ptolemy he was playing with fire. The sixteenth century in Europe was a dangerous time to say or write anything that went against the teachings of the Church. Doing so risked torture on the rack or burning at the stake. He died of natural causes soon after he published his ideas and so was spared such a fate.

Galileo Galilei was born some twenty years after the death of Copernicus. Early in the seventeenth century Galileo improved upon the spyglass invented in Flanders. Increasing its magnification some ten-fold he built the first telescope, and turned it away from the trading and navigational concerns of the Venetian state and towards the heavens, thus ushering in the beginnings of the era of modern astronomy. In addition to mapping the moon's surface, discovering some of the satellites of Jupiter, and seeing for the first time stars in numbers never recorded before, he was able with certainty to see that Ptolemy had been wrong and Copernicus right.

Galileo was a wonderful scientist and mathematician, perhaps the first person that could be described as a scientist in the modern sense of that word. But he made the mistake of making his findings and thoughts too public at a time when the Catholic Church was launching a furious counter-attack on the rise of the Protestant reformation. One consequence was a ferocious resistance to the idea that the universe could be understood outside of Divine law, and science, albeit it embryonic science, was seen flagrantly to flout this edict. The fate Copernicus feared very nearly fell upon Galileo. In 1633 Galileo was brought to trial by the Holy Roman and Universal Inquisition. Threatened with the instruments of torture he was frightened and humiliated, and forced to retract his claim that Copernicus' model had been correct.

Never again was a scientist or scholar of Galileo's eminence tortured or threatened with torture for holding and communicating ideas that ran counter to religious doctrine. Newton, Priestly, Lavoisier, and Dalton, amongst many others, were subsequently allowed to ply their trades in relative freedom of action, and even of censure, from authorities of any kind. Never again were astronomy, physics, and chemistry seriously trammeled by ideology or religion. More mundane social sanction, however, is a powerful force, and biology, especially those parts of biology concerned with the human mind, remained vulnerable to potent criticism not just only from official religious quarters but from a more general public consensus. Planets and their orbits are one thing. Living creatures and the minds of humans are quite another.

There is a pervasive view, present to this day, that life is a gift from the Divine and that our minds are a special instrument that allows us an awareness of God the Creator. Even that most extraordinary feature of the human mind, our intelligence, has been thought of as existing in order that we may comprehend God's law and adhere to it, or otherwise, with appropriate consequences in the afterlife. Most modern scientists are thoroughgoing materialists convinced that living things, including human minds, are nothing more than physics and chemistry, albeit very complex physics and chemistry. The average nonscientist in industrialized societies is, perhaps, coming to a similar view, if much troubled by how to deal with consciousness. But this is a very modern phenomenon. And even major scientists in the none-too-distant past were adherents to nonmaterialist beliefs. For example, Johannes Müller was a major figure in nineteenth-century German physiology, and hence as will become clear in a later chapter, of great significance to early psychology. Yet throughout his career Muller subscribed to a form of vitalism, believing in a nonmaterial essence of life and conscious mind. Similarly Hans Driesch, an important nineteenth-century embryologist, was a persistent and influential purveyor of the view that a purely materialist approach to any science of life would never be enough. Some kind of *elan vital* or *entelechy*, to use Aristotle's phrase, is an essential part of any and every living thing. Alfred Russell Wallace no less, codiscoverer with Darwin of the process of natural selection, had some starkly nonmaterialist ideas about both the human mind and human evolution. That such views increasingly lost the respect of fellow scientists is beside the point. Many biologists in the nineteenth and twentieth centuries, especially evolutionists and that includes Charles Darwin, performed at times what might be termed "attitudinal acrobatics" in order not to offend the traditional public view that if the divine cannot easily be seen in the cosmos, it certainly can be apprehended in living things, and particularly so in the human mind. No evolutionist or psychologist has ever received the treatment meted out to Galileo. But without wishing to labor the point, it is worth noting that the center of twentieth-century science, the United States of America, was home in that century to two major legal battles about the teaching of evolution science, the second as recently as the early 1980s. In 1999 the state of Kansas withdrew evolutionary theory from its schools curriculum and several states, like Washington, are preparing to take similar moves now in the beginnings of the twenty-first century.

All of this makes a simple point. As will be seen, the histories of psychology and evolutionary biology are in many ways curiously parallel. Scientific psychology, in the sense of an empirically based discipline, and the Darwinian theory of evolution, both came into the world at approximately the same time, from about 1860–75. Both had long nonscientific provenances. Speculation about the nature of the mind, either as complex narrative dilemmas and morality tales as in the writings of Homer or as philosophical analysis which predates Plato (427–347 B.C.), are as old as recorded history. Nor did evolution come to us first through Darwin with the publication in 1859 of his *The Origin of Species*. A number of philosophers and naturalists of the eighteenth century had toyed with the notion of the nonfixity of species; Lamarck had developed the first ever substantive theory of the transformation of species at the start of the nineteenth century; and something approximating to a functional theory in the form of final causes and teleological analysis, as well as vague ideas of universal relatedness of all living things, is present in the writings of Aristotle (384–322 B.C.). Also, both evolution and psychology are profoundly important to how humans see themselves. Thus when both achieved the status of being sciences, both were assailed by the world outside of each discipline, especially the theory of evolution. Both have also been riven by internal schisms and controversies. Psychology in particular has always been a refractory area of science. From its empirical beginnings in Germany in the mid-nineteenth century, psychologists themselves, as well as other prominent nineteenth-century social philosophers, held that the human mind had to be approached in two fundamentally different ways. On the one hand, there is the stuff of sensation, attention, learning and memory which can be studied as science through normal, if ingenious, empirical methodology. These are things that can be measured and experimentally manipulated. On the other hand, there was *Homo sapiens* as a social and conscious being whose essence could only be understood by interpretation of meaning – and which certainly cannot be measured. Are these even the same disciplines? Evolutionary science, in turn, suffered major divisions in terms both of theories and methodologies. The differences, deep differences, between Lamarkians and Darwinians, especially as these respective theories were applied to humans, had, as will be seen, a profound and damaging impact on the naturalizing of the social sciences. As to whether a science rooted in history is even a science at all was not the kind of insulting question posed for more traditional natural sciences like chemistry or physiology.

But it is in the treading about as close as science can come to ideology that the most important shared feature lies. How humans should view themselves, and hence how best we should live our lives, is a burden that weighs heavily upon both disciplines and is, and always has been, a source of serious contention, both internally as well as being directed from outside of each science. So when people began, a few decades ago, to run the two sciences together, the effect was explosive and bitterly controversial.

That is the simple point referred to above. While there never has been an equivalent case to that of Galileo in either psychology or evolutionary biology – not even in so-called evolutionary psychology – these are sciences which, when compared with the likes of chemistry or physics over the same period of time, from about 1860 onwards, have been battered by extrascientific ideas and events; and many of those in the thick of the arguments have been influenced by external events far more than is common in most areas of science.

There is another feature in this most curious of histories of evolutionary ideas within psychology. This is that apart from the earliest period of their joint establishment as sciences of one kind or another, that is evolutionary biology on the one hand and psychology on the other, until quite recently, these were two areas of human thought that had little contact with one another. That is, psychology, whether of humans or animals, had almost no presence within evolutionary biology. And evolutionary theory in its various aspects played little or no part in the thinking of the great majority of academic psychologists. Indeed, there is good reason for this. Because of the empiricist origins of psychological science in western intellectual history as opposed to the inclination towards nativism within evolutionary theory, there has always been the tendency for each to see the other as a rival account of the human mind. Whilst this separation has never been absolute and complete it has always been a division between the two, and one that remains to a large extent. The empiricists lay stress upon the importance of experience in shaping minds, be they human or nonhuman. Nativists (or rationalists in more traditional philosophical language) emphasize that much of human nature is inborn. That greatest of all rationalists, Plato, even believed that human knowledge is innate. Impelled along their separate conceptual courses by so profound a difference as this, ideas about the evolution of mind have long been at odds with those coming from most academic psychologists.

Yet the views of outsiders have been otherwise. Human origins have always been of powerful interest to people at large. So too is the workings of the human mind. Running the two together in recent years has led to unprecedented media interest. Any linkage that can be established between the mind and our origins is widely felt to be at once fascinating and important, and has attracted public interest way beyond the importance accorded to it by insiders. Nor has the intense interest been confined to that famous person on the Clapham omnibus. Fellow academics and scholars, especially philosophers, have evinced similar enthusiasm.

There is a further complicating thread that needs to be woven into the complex fabric of a history of evolutionary thinking within psychology. This is that there have been, and continue to be, two ways of bringing evolution into psychology. The one is by way of the "standard" evolutionary idea that many features of humankind, perhaps most, including the structure and function of our minds, are a product of evolutionary forces. We are the way we are because of the evolutionary history of our species. The other is that evolutionary processes operate both within our minds as well as between them, an idea sometimes referred to as universal Darwinism. We are the way we are because there is a common set of processes that governs the transformation of living systems, be it the change in species in geological time or alterations in the memories and thoughts of an individual within their lifetime. As will be seen, the relationship between these two notions is not simple.

One of the distinctions historians of science make is between intellectual history and more socially oriented accounts. Intellectual histories are concerned only with the ways in which factors intrinsic to a science have determined its course. The interplay between theory and data, the way in which new methodologies have led to deeper reaches within the phenomena under study, and improvements in theory by recasting and reanalyzing existing theories relative to the findings from empirical study, all these are grist to the intellectual historical mill of how sciences have changed over the years. Social accounts concentrate on how scientists are affected by, and are products of, the social circumstances of their lives and the times in which they live; and hence how science, and hence the history of science, is the product of such external social and ideological forces. Now, claims upon truth are always precarious if not plain foolhardy. But the prevailing view amongst most scientists is that science does gradually move towards some kind of truth about the world. The astonishing success of science and its application, which ranges from placing humans on the moon and soon enough on Mars too, to linking human nervous systems to computers, and on to cloning, is some sort of measure of truth. Thus most **scientists** writing history would incline to an intellectual perspective, believing that insofar as science is truth-seeking, it does so under the harsh disciplines of accuracy of observations, the adequacy of theory to explain them, and the ingenuity of their application. Yet no scientist is immune to the effects of their lives outside of science on their thinking within their science. And when their science sails close to the ideological winds of what it means to be human, which is what both human evolution and psychology do, then some degree of awareness of a social perspective must be allowed to enter the picture. What follows, then, is largely an intellectual history. But external social forces cannot be left out, and where they seem relevant they will be considered.

All of this means that any history of evolutionary ideas within psychology faces structural problems. What we have here are two difficult, cantankerous, edgy and socially vulnerable sciences which have two rather different ways of relating to one another. Apart from an initial period dating from around 1870 to the turn of the twentieth century when there was a relationship, if tenuous and relatively ungrounded conceptually, evolution and psychology had little to say to one another through much of the twentieth century. Then things began to change, but the engines driving this change came from sciences neighboring upon psychology, and not from psychology itself. *This is because evolutionary theory only effectively enters psychology when specific aspects of the theory drive empirical studies and frame causal explanations.* This will be referred to as the principle of specific application. In the nineteenth century a vague notion of continuity between species formed the less than robust basis for considering the evolution of the human mind. During the first half of the twentieth century no credible basis at all was presented for thinking of the workings of the mind in evolutionary terms. Then from the 1950s into the 1980s ethology and sociobiology emerged with strong claims to understanding the behavior of animals in evolutionary terms. Following overzealous applications of these ideas to humans came a more focused, more cautious (in the main, though with some notably reckless exceptions), more specific insertion of evolutionary thinking into psychology. The result now is a more defensible, if still minority, and still controversial, view that evolutionary theory can be gainfully applied to the study and understanding of the human mind.

That, then, is how this history proceeds. It is largely intellectual, though not wholly so. It runs two parallel lines of thought and theory, the mind as product of evolution versus the mind as a Darwin machine, with an attempt to show how these relate to one another and how they do not. And it runs the history in roughly chronological order. But the history of evolutionary thought in psychology has a curious shape. There is something, perhaps not much that impinges upon contemporary theory but historically an important something, to tell about the nineteenth century. Then there is relatively little to say about the first and largest part of the twentieth century. Here there is a gaping, and intellectually shameful, hole in the body of psychological theory. After that there is the need to switch disciplines slightly, with a return to psychology proper from the 1980s to the present. Because the time covered is, to the historian, very limited, there is no disguising the fact that this is not a history that can fruitfully apportion equal space to equal time periods over the last two hundred years. We will begin at the beginning, which is in the years before Darwin, because it was in that pre-Darwinian era that important mistakes were made that took decades to put right and which, in some ways, echo through to the present.

CHAPTER TWO

Before Darwin

There is no beginning to the history of human thought. This is a consequence of what is, perhaps, the single defining feature of our species, the only characteristic that is uniquely human. We are creatures of culture, but a culture like that of no other animal, which results in the thought of any one human being so closely bound up with that of the thought of others that we can have no way of knowing when or where any one begins and another ends. It presents anyone writing a history of ideas with a problem. Where to start? In the case of the history of evolution and the human mind, many choose René Descartes (1596–1650) because as the father of modern philosophy he drove distinctions between mind and matter, and between humans and nonhumans, that have drawn clear lines of thought ever since. But equally, one can go back two thousand years before Renaissance Europe to a question which is certainly more fundamental than anything raised by Descartes when placed within the specific context of the history of mind and evolution. It was posed by Plato in the opening lines of the *Meno*: "Can you tell me, Socrates – can virtue be taught, or is it rather to be acquired by practice? Or is it neither to be practised nor learned, but something that comes to men by nature or in some other way?" This is the archetypal casting of the nature–nurture issue which continues to dominate psychology today, and which is at the heart of how best to bring evolutionary theory into an understanding of the human mind.

Given the connectedness of human thought and the limitations of space in a small book, where one begins, and what is emphasized, is determined by the aims of this chapter. This is the writings of two men, Jean-Baptiste de Lamarck (1774–1829) and Herbert Spencer (1820–1903). Plato and Descartes were giants of philosophy. Lamarck and Spencer were certainly not. Indeed Spencer is much derided today and likely to merit no more than a footnote in histories of nineteenth-century thought. Lamarck was a biologist of great significance, even if his ideas on evolution, which constituted the first real theory of how evolution occurs, were entirely wrong. But what Lamarck and Spencer have in common is that their work sowed the seeds of discord that so damaged the advance of evolutionary thought in psychology and the other social sciences for decades. Spencer was a follower of Lamarck and hence both were believers in the transformation of species. But neither Lamarck nor Spencer are direct products of any specific lineages of ideas, either philosophical or biological. For that reason, the pre-Darwinian scene must be set within a rather general framework.

Preliminaries

In the immediate aftermath of the publication of Darwin's main works, those thinking and writing about the mind and evolution most often focused on the similarities and differences between humans and other animals. To a degree, the fascination with comparisons between human and nonhuman animals is still with us. But in the seventeenth and eighteenth centuries such comparisons were a major preoccupation with those writing about the mind – that is, the human mind. In his excellent account of the history of evolutionary theories of mind and behavior, Robert Richards, an American historian, argues that three different schools of thought attracted supporters during this relatively early period. There were the Aristotelians, the Cartesians, and the sensationalists. For our purposes, the Aristotelians and the Cartesians can be collapsed into a single school since, whilst the former presented a more mystical conception bound up with notions of human and animal souls whereas the Cartesians were much more down-to-earth and mechanistic in approach, they were united in the common view that much of animal behavior, in particular complex behavior patterns (honey bee nest constructions as well as complicated behaviors of other social insects, and the building of nests by birds were examples repeatedly used) are explicable in terms of instincts whereas the mind of man is marked by rational powers. The sensationalists, by contrast, adhered to the empiricist philosophy of John Locke.

There is much to be sorted out and explained here, with Aristoteleans raising the specter of classical Greek philosophy. However, this is not a philosophical tract, and indeed not much of pre-Cartesian philosophy bears in any very strong or direct way on the main theme of this book. Two issues raised by Plato (427–347 B.C.) and Aristotle (384–322 B.C.), though, are important. These are, first, whether knowledge is in some way inborn or innate (which, as will be repeatedly pointed out, is in part a rephrasing of the nature–nurture question because resolution of that question hinges upon the existence or nonexistence of innate knowledge), and second, how to think about causation. So while the philosophy, especially that from before Descartes, will be kept as brief as possible, and vast tracts of both Plato and Aristotle will be omitted, these two major issues are very major indeed, and for this reason a brief visit must be paid to ancient Greek philosophy.

In the same dialogue, the *Meno*, in which Plato asked his question on the origins of virtue, and answered in terms of the nature–nurture dichotomy that has so bedeviled the human sciences ever since, is also one of his most famous expositions of his view that knowledge is innate. What Plato has Socrates do in this dialogue is to question a young slave about problems in geometry, and in so doing, the slave reveals that he has knowledge of geometry that he was not previously aware of, and in which he had never before received formal tuition.

Two points need to be made at once. The first is that Plato was limiting himself to some very specific forms of knowledge. In positing knowledge to be a form of reminiscence in which remembering is facilitated by appropriate training, as in the learning of logic and mathematics, Plato does not have Socrates expecting the slave to have come into the world knowing the name of his father or the birthplace of his mother. What Plato considers to be knowledge is defined by its *a priori* form. That some quantity is greater than another, or that two things are equal, is the kind of knowledge Plato is invoking. Specific experiential and referential knowledge is not what he was referring to. That a certain distance is called a mile and another distance is referred to as a kilometer is irrelevant. What matters is that the former is greater than the latter. And that what I hold in one hand is a kilogram which I judge to be the same as what I have in the other, which is 2.2 pounds, is equally beside the point. That I judge them to be the same is what counts. It is the understanding, the knowledge, of relative quantity or of equality that exists independently of experience that matters. The concepts of "greater or lesser than" and "this is equal to that" is what Plato is considering as innate. This is an important philosophical stance known as rationalism, and it has been one of the polar positions adopted by some in scientific psychology across a range of psychological phenomena.

The second point to note is that in order to maintain his rationalist stance, Plato had to have a way by which knowledge is transmitted between individuals other than that which comes from tuition. That, after all, was his point. *A priori* knowledge is knowledge that precedes experience. It must, nonetheless, have a source. This is where Plato's mysticism has a role to play. Plato, in the view of some, is the greatest philosopher of all times. But to the modern nonspecialist reader he held some very strange beliefs. One of these is a consistent dualism of thought, which includes that of soul and body, and a belief in reincarnation. Plato, like his teacher Socrates (history, to repeat, has no beginnings), believed that death operates to separate the body from the soul, which is different from, and altogether superior to the body. The latter is corrupt and unreliable, and a positive hindrance to the acquisition of knowledge. Sight and hearing, as with all of the senses, are a part of the body, and hence not trustworthy sources of knowledge. For Plato "the body is the source of endless trouble... having got rid of the foolishness of the body we shall be pure and have converse with the pure, and know of ourselves the clear light everywhere, which is no other than the light of truth." If truth is revealed to the soul, it is done so in thought, not experience. The senses are thus to be ignored, or sidestepped. What reveals truth are ideas bound up with mathematics and logic; the real world is the world of ideas, and since reality is bound up with "the good" (and understanding precisely what "the good" is, is something of a holy grail for Platonists), ideas are what are important and the eventual revealers of true knowledge. And because the soul exists before birth, Plato believing in a form of reincarnation, our knowledge comes to us before birth by way of the reincarnated soul. Hence the notion of knowledge as reminiscence.

This may sound like mystical gobbledy-gook to many modern readers (though certainly not all), but it does represent a very important core question that pervades psychology: are some forms of human knowledge innate?

Aristotle, though a pupil of Plato and influenced by him at least within the context of the teacher-pupil relationship (another example of history without beginning), presents a very different kind of philosophy. Modern science may begin with Galileo, but Aristotle is surely the father of all science. He contributed to studies of logic and metaphysics and methods of gaining knowledge. Above all, though, he originated systematic study by observing and ordering his observations. He wrote on physics and about a quarter of his work concerned biology. He described the anatomy of hundreds of species of animals and, along the way, provided the first detailed descriptions of complex behavior in nonhuman species. Aristotle was also the first philosopher to write on psychology, though his work bears little relationship to the modern form of this discipline. He believed that a fundamental distinction of the natural world is between the animate and the inanimate, with the former possessing a psyche (hence the word psychology), or soul. There is some argument amongst experts on Aristotle's work as to how far he meant the notion of "soul" to be an attribute of any and every living thing. He seemed to solve the problem for himself by arguing that soul was made up of a number of different "powers," and that plants, for instance, have only nutritive powers, with increasing powers of perception, movement, inclination, thought, and intelligence in animals forming a scale of increasing complexity, thus formulating the beginnings of what later would be called the *scala naturae*. He differed from Plato in denying that the soul could be separated from the body, but with one important exception which does indeed smack of Plato: thought is divine and comes "from the outside," but not, as in Plato's system from the souls of others.

There is one other major difference, for our purposes, between Plato and Aristotle. One of Aristotle's most famous achievements was the invention of formal deductive logic. Whilst one would reasonably consider Aristotle's formal logic system to be a prime example of knowledge in Plato's sense, for Aristotle, perception, information from the senses, is an absolutely essential part of knowledge. Aristotle was as much an empiricist as a rationalist.

One other contribution was made by Aristotle, which is the second major issue referred to above, whose importance lies in its central role in modern evolutionary biology. This was his analysis of causation. Believing that successful science depends upon an understanding of cause, Aristotle presented a scheme of four forms of causation. The first is material cause or cause "as matter." This book is caused by the paper and ink dyes of which it is made, and hence imparts particular qualities to it, like its being likely to tear or smudge. The second form of cause is efficient cause, the causes by which something comes into existence, which comes close to an everyday as well as a standard scientific understanding of causation. The causes of this book is a long sequence of events which include its original conception and writing, the process of making paper from wood pulp, the translation of the written (or computer processed) word onto the printed page, and so on. Aristotle's third cause, formal cause, is rather more obscure. It is the essence of a thing – in this specific case, an instance of a book that seeks to trace the history of evolutionary thinking in psychology. It is his fourth cause that is of most importance to us, which is the "final" or "end" cause – the goal of something. It is easy enough to infer goals for human artifacts. The goal of this small book is to impart to others a particular view about the history of evolutionary thought in psychology. But Aristotle conceived of final causes as applying to all things, including the inanimate. For him everything, living or nonliving, is subject to a finalistic form-giving force that drives everything to a state of perfection. Again we have a form of mysticism in its original conception, if one which is easy to reconcile with subsequent religious doctrine. But unlike material or efficient causes, Aristotelian finalism, end-directed cause, or what is sometimes referred to as teleological thinking, is not easy to fit with scientific analysis prior to the nineteenth century. In effect, it places effects before their causes, and this violates *a posteriori* causation which is the bedrock of standard scientific thinking (at least prior to the era of contemporary physics where time can run backwards). Yet in thinking about living creatures, teleological thinking seems both easy and significant. The reason why birds have hollow bones is that their hollowness is "for" the reduction of weight and hence the facilitation of flight. The large slashing teeth of carnivores is "for" the easy disabling and killing of prey. Well, Darwin, asserts Ernst Mayr who is one of the greatest of living evolutionists, solved the problem of teleology (as will be seen in the next chapter). He gave it scientific respectability for the first time in the two thousand and more years since Aristotle had introduced the concept. The Darwinian resolution of the apparent end-directedness of many behaviors which **seem** *a priori* also provides the basis of an explanation for innate knowledge, as will be seen in a later chapter. And as already stated, the issue of innate knowledge is inseparable from the nature–nurture problem.

Aristotle's writings cover an astonishing range of subjects and his work held a preeminent place in the subsequent development of European thought. It is no surprise that seventeenth- and eighteenth-century scholars included a school of Aristoteleans much influenced by his ideas, including their application to animal behavior. His work was also accepted by the Church whose teachings of an omniscient and omnipotent God chimed well with Aristotelian finalism. Scholars propagating his ideas did not risk censure. This cannot be said for Descartes who, though a devout Catholic, was utterly committed to telling the truth as he saw it, and who lived and worked in an age of much turmoil when the rise of science, as in the case of Galileo, was seen to threaten the doctrines of the Church. Descartes was a rationalist, like Plato, who considered sensory experience to be untrustworthy. No confidence, he asserted, can be had in evidence from the senses: we might be dreaming, hallucinating, drugged, or even had our thoughts taken over by an evil demon. Thus, the content of thought is suspect. But not the ability to think itself. Hence his famous *cogito, ergo sum* – thought is all that we can be certain of as proof that we exist and are different from all other things, and if there is such a thing as certain knowledge, it comes only through the exercise of reason.

Descartes' arguments led him to two clear conclusions. The first, and much the most famous, is that the mind and the body are entirely different and separate. This is the dualist thesis, which was wholly reasonable to most people in Descartes' time, and remains so today to many. Mind stuff or thinking substance, *res cogitans*, has no physical extension and cannot be measured; this is in contrast to *res extensa*, which has properties like size or weight and which can be measured. Most scientists, however, reject dualism. This is no place to review the mind–body problem and the many solutions that have been offered to solve it. Suffice it to say that to the materialist or physicalist, which is what almost all scientists are, it is inconceivable that the mind should somehow be wholly different in kind from the body.

Descartes second conclusion was that no animal has mind. They all, of course, have *res extensa*, and that includes some very complex behaviors in some species, but none have the rational capacities of man which can be communicated by language. Nonhuman animals are beast-machines whose actions are automatic and inborn – instinctive. Descartes even considered the possibility of building a machine that behaved like a human and pondered on how one could distinguish such a device from "the real thing," thus anticipating by several hundred years the kinds of arguments and analysis that the age of computers ushered in during the twentieth century. This was not as utterly fanciful on his part as might first be thought. Descartes had been much impressed by the "animated" statues in some French gardens in which a god-like Neptune might be made to appear from behind foliage or disappear under water on the basis of levers operating valves which, in turn, would result in a flow of water allowing the placement and displacement of figures in a seemingly complex inanimate choreography. Why, asked Descartes, might not something very similar be happening in the nervous systems of animals, and of humans in the case of automated, instinctive behaviors, whereby spirits are routed along the nerve tracts to muscles. Why not indeed? This is the beginnings of an account of actions in terms of reflexes, which in time was to acquire a solid physiological basis of explanation.

Descartes' beast-machine proved a provocative vision. Julian Offray de la Mettrie (1709–51), a French physician whose experiences of human beastliness in time of war led him to doubt the absolute difference between humans and beasts imposed by Descartes, extended the Cartesian beast-machine to account for the human mind as well. La Mettrie could not see why human thought and learning should not be considered automatic and unconscious and be an expression of the activity of *res extensa*. In a, perhaps, weak sense, all is instinct. Nor could he discern a higher moral sense in humans when compared to animals. Humans **are** machines; and we **are** animals. Some of these ideas are remarkably ahead of their time and one must conclude that la Mettrie had a singular intelligence. He published his ideas in 1748, in a volume entitled "L'homme machine." It was over a century since Galileo had had to face the Inquisition, yet such was the danger of his views to the church, and hence to himself, that la Mettrie had to flee Holland, where he was then living, for Berlin where he was given sanctuary provided he kept himself busy with less troublesome topics, like the causes of asthma.

It should be said that the Cartesian or Aristotelian usage of the word "instinct" does not in any way carry any of the connotations of genetic cause or biological determinism that it does now. When used in the seventeenth and eighteenth centuries, instinct merely meant behavior that is impulsive, automatic and not guided by thought – in effect, beast-like.

We are left with one last preliminary matter, and that is the opposing position of the sensationalists, and their roots in British empiricism. The rise of science, especially Newtonian physics, in the late seventeenth and early eighteenth centuries, raised serious doubts about the rationalist view that the senses are unreliable sources of knowledge. This is because science rests on observation of the world, and however indirect that observation might become as complex instruments intervene between the phenomena observed and the scientist-observer, in the end that observation occurs by way of the senses. It is no coincidence that Aristotle, the great philosopher-scientist who spent so much of his life observing and describing the world, should have broken with his teacher's strict adherence to a rationalist philosophy of knowledge and insisted that knowledge begins, at least in part, in perception. If the establishment by scientists of ever better instruments to improve the accuracy of their observation shows anything, it is not a distrust in the truth that comes to us by our senses, enhanced by instruments if need be, but in the extent to which we can come to knowledge via our senses with something approaching the precision demanded by science. Doubting the accuracy of the knowledge that comes to us by way of our unenhanced senses is not to doubt that what we see, hear or feel is at least an approximation to truth and not forever hopelessly disengaged from it.

As with Aristotle, so with the earliest of the empiricist philosophers of the sixteenth and seventeenth centuries. Bacon and Locke identified themselves with the rise of early modern science which was intensely practical, rather than theoretical – despite the enormous power, and hence importance, of Newton's theory.

Ideas were not enough. They had to be based on observation and they had to do work in practical terms.

John Locke (1632–1704) was one of the founders of the empiricist movement. Locke attended Oxford University, trained for a time as a physician, and numbered some of the great scientists of his day, like Robert Boyle and Isaac Newton, amongst his acquaintances. He was also a politically active figure who had to flee England for a time. Thus his philosophy was far from being confined to matters of knowledge. But as with previous figures treated in these preliminary notes, neither time nor relevance allows for consideration beyond his epistemology, that is the philosophy of whether and how knowledge is possible, and the certainty we can attribute to our knowledge. Locke's central thesis was quite simple. All knowledge is based upon experience. There are no innate ideas and no innate processes by which knowledge is organized. In the second book of his *Essay Concerning Human Understanding* he wrote:

> Let us then suppose the mind to be, as we say, white paper, void of all characters, without any ideas: how comes it to be furnished? Whence comes it by that vast store, which the busy and boundless fancy of man has painted on it with an almost endless variety? Whence has it all the materials of reason and knowledge? To this I answer in one word, from experience: in that all our knowledge is founded, and from that it ultimately derives itself. (In Nidditch, 1975, Book, II, Chapter 1, Section 2, p. 48)

This is the statement of the famous blank slate or *tabula rasa*, and has proved, especially following the founding of scientific psychology some two centuries later, one of the most enduring and contentious axioms of the science and philosophy of knowledge. Locke's ideas were allied closely to Newton's physics, which is one of the reasons for its success. For a time Cartesian rationalism was eclipsed and it took a full century before the writings of Immanuel Kant provided an epistemology that resurrected certain aspects of the rationalist thesis.

David Hume (1711–76) was an intellectual descendent of Locke. He believed that human knowledge could and should be considered within the context of a science of humanity with a science of mind being based upon the model of Newtonian physics – a kind of mental mechanics. Like Locke he rejected the notion of innate knowledge, believing that "there is no idea without antecedent impression," by which he meant that all knowledge begins at the sensory surfaces. Sensations and perceptions give rise to ideas, and ideas become associated through regular, lawful processes. Understand the laws of association and you have understanding of how humans come to have knowledge. These last two sentences were never uttered in that way by Hume, but they capture his meaning and also depict the central belief of twentieth-century associationist psychology. It might also be noted that Hume had some startling things to say about the human understanding of cause–effect relationship. He considered that our tendency to structure the world in terms of causes and their effects was less a reflection of the real structure of the world, and more a matter of habit of thought combining both associationist tendencies and the propensity to exercise reasoning by induction. In this too Hume anticipates associationist psychology.

Thus we arrive at some understanding of the sensationalist doctrine. It was based on two premises. The first was the openly empiricist view that knowledge is born of sensation, and that rational intelligence of the kind Descartes had pointed to is the result of complex processes of association. Instincts are not inborn but acquired by experience. The second is that if animals are machines, as Descartes taught, why then so too are humans. Just as human knowledge is the accrual of ever more complex associations of ideas, so too does this occur in animals. It should be pointed out that the rise of sensationalism was connected to Enlightenment philosophy. If all knowledge is acquired and none inborn, then under appropriate circumstances of social engineering of the human environment all people would stand as equal in their knowledge, and hence in their abilities. "Inferior" peoples could be made the true equals of all people. La Mettrie even mused upon the consequences of teaching language to an orangutan using the same methods by which communication is taught to the deaf, suggesting that the outcome would be a perfect little gentleman (a female orang, presumably, would not do). This is precisely what psychologist began to attempt in the 1960s, though the results were not those predicted by la Mettrie.

Readers may be inclined to throw their hands in the air and ask how the glaringly obvious differences between diverse nonhuman animals could be so easily ignored, or why the even more evident differences between humans and all other animals could be so easily cast aside. This seems an especially pertinent question in the light of the way some sensationalists mocked the Cartesian position by asking how anyone who has ever owned a dog could consider them as mere machines, a tacit appeal to evidence of some kind. The answer is simply that nobody in that age was doing science. No one was observing, collating, and weighing the evidence with any care or consistency, much less doing experiments, to settle the matter. La Mettrie did not attempt to train an orangutan. He simply speculated on the likely outcome were it to be done. However, a further point should be made. Language remained, in the minds of many, the key difference between humans and other animals, whatever la Mettrie concluded from his musings. And if one species could acquire knowledge in a realm unavailable to all others, which (to repeat the crucial point) is what defines humans, then this has profound consequences for any theory of knowledge. Nobody at that time seemed to see how important to the argument even one form of knowledge unique to one species is. This, too, is a point to be returned to later in this book.

One vigorous exponent of sensationalism was Erasmus Darwin (1731–1802), grandfather of Charles Darwin. In many respects his views on animal behavior were no different from others. He rejected the Cartesian notion of the beast-machine and instincts, and fully embraced the empiricist doctrine of the association of ideas. But in one respect he was different from most sensationalists, if not exactly original. Like a growing number of scholars, Erasmus Darwin was a transformationist. That is, he did not believe that species were fixed in form for all time. In short, he was an evolutionist.

Jean-Baptiste de Lamarck

George-Louis Leclerc Buffon's *Histoire Naturelle* was perhaps the most widely read natural science writing of the eighteenth century. In his *Histoire*, which comprised many volumes written over several decades, Buffon anticipated many of the advances biology was to make over the next one hundred years:

> If it were admitted that the ass is of the family of the horse, and different from the horse only because it has varied from the

original form, one could equally well say that the ape is of the family of man, that he is a degenerate man, that man and ape have a common origin; that, in fact, all the families, among plants as well as animals, have come from a single stock, and that all animals are descended from a single animal, from which have sprung in the course of time, as a result of progress or of degeneration, all the other races of animals. (In Mayr, 1982, p. 332)

Buffon wrote this in 1766, and this is as close as one can get to a statement of the transformation of species originating from a single living source. Buffon, though not an evolutionist in any consistent sense, was not alone in his flirtation with the idea that the earth and all its living forms was not created fully and finally formed just a few thousand years before the birth of Christ. Erasmus Darwin in England was singing the same tune, as were a number of other European, especially French, thinkers. Bonnet and Maupertuis are other names to add to that of Buffon, and Kant is often added to the list because he dared to consider time as having no beginning and no end, or at least that earthly time is to be measured in tens of millions of years. This is an absolutely crucial point. If species were not fixed in form, and had not all been created at the same time as in the biblical account, then great swathes of time would be needed for species to have changed.

As the nineteenth century progressed geologists did indeed begin to open up the possibility of a history of our planet extending over tens or even hundreds of millions of years. But there was also accumulating evidence from other sources that nudged naturalists towards the view that species are not fixed in form. The founder of taxonomy, Carl Linnaeus who himself developed a kind of evolutionary theory, in the mid-eighteenth century estimated that there were 20,000 extant species of animals and plants. Within decades this number had increased to hundreds of thousands, and then to millions. (Contemporary estimates range from around ten to forty million species all told; and we now know that the earth is about 4.6 thousand million years old.) Also, the new science of fossils was revealing a picture quite at odds with a biblical account of the origins of life. It was known with certainty that some species, like mammoths, that once existed had become extinct. Well, if creation had occurred around 4,000 B.C. as a "single act," and if some species had since died out, the diversity of living forms should have reduced, not increased, but the fossil record showed that the latter was what had occurred. What was more, recent fossils resembled living forms more than did older fossils. Buffon's musings about descent from a single source seemed less and less outrageous as the eighteenth turned into the nineteenth century.

Buffon has a further role to play in this story. In the mid-1770s he secured the services of a young man, whose name was Jean Lamarck and who was much interested in biology, especially botany, to be tutor and companion to his son. In 1788 Buffon, whose influence in France was enormous, secured for Lamarck a position as a botanical assistant at the natural history museum and after just five years, as a result of his prodigious energy and productivity, Lamarck was appointed professor of "inferior" animals (i.e. invertebrates). In 1799 Lamarck was not yet an evolutionist, according to Ernst Mayr. By 1800 he had changed and embraced an evolutionary position, which was published in book form in 1809 in his *Philosophie Zoologique*. The cause of this conversion to a transformationist stance is not certain, but Mayr and others believe that it was his meticulous study of fossil and living mollusks (animals like snails and mussels) which persuaded him that here was incontrovertible proof of the gradual change of species in time.

What made Lamarck different from, say, Erasmus Darwin, was that Lamarck presented a much more substantial if informal theory of how and why evolution occurs; what in modern parlance would be called a process-based account of evolution. Lamarck's starting assumptions were that organisms are always wonderfully well adapted to their environments, but also that environments constantly change in time. From these it followed that organisms themselves must be able to change in time. How this occurs is the core of Lamarck's theory, and it has two parts. The first is that as the environment changes it imposes new needs on the organisms within it; these needs result in changes in activity and it is these alterations in activity that result in modifications to bodily structures. Known as the law of use and disuse, what Lamarck envisaged was that the more used and exercised a body part was, the greater would be its growth and transformation; the less used and exercised structures would reduce and even disappear. This "principle" was married to that of the inheritance of acquired characters, which stated that such structural changes would be passed on to offspring. Whilst the second of these principles is often invoked as the epitomy of Lamarckian theory, it is in fact an unoriginal idea that dates back to ancient Greek philosophy.

Lamarck's was less a theory of descent, as it became in Darwin's hands, and more one of ascent because governing the operation of these processes is the tendency of all living things to change from simple and imperfect forms to states of increasing complexity and perfection. Here again we have the notion of the *scala naturae* with life beginning continuously and spontaneously in slimes and molds, and progressing via his principles of use and disuse and the inheritance of acquired characters through intermediate stages of complexity and perfection to arrive finally at its most complex and perfect form, us – human beings.

A contemporary of Lamarck, Pierre-Jean Cabanis, had arrived at a very similar theory, even though evolutionists now hardly know of him. It is Lamarck's name that carries the fame. Yet in certain respects Cabanis' theory was clearer than that of Lamarck, particularly as it addressed the old and vexed issue of instinct. Cabanis recognized that animals do come into the world with certain behavioral tendencies, and that a rigid sensationalist denial of inborn behavioral propensities was not adequate. But what Cabanis saw clearly was that any theory like Lamarck's lays great stress on behavior. It would be wrong to assert that changes in the world which exert altered needs on organisms can only be compensated for by changes in behavior, but there is little doubt that Lamarck's and Cabanis' position gave prominence to behavioral responses to environmental change. Despite Cabanis' recognition of some degree of innate behavioral tendencies he still embraced the sensationalist emphasis on the importance of learning of some kind, associationist or otherwise, in the shaping of adult behavior. So, if behavioral change is one of the engines that drives the transformation of species, and if such behavioral change is driven at least in part by learning of whatever sort, then the role of learning becomes a factor in evolution itself. The precise relationship between learning and instinct also moves to center stage. As will be seen, all this becomes a major theme in the history of ideas about mind and evolution.

One last point is worth making about Lamarck's theory. It is essentially a theory of **progress** by way of the interplay of specified processes of environmental change, organismic needs and activity giving rise to changes within organisms that are passed across generations. Progress is a word redolent with social meaning. A provocative scientific theory on the transformation of species, set squarely on a collision course with traditional beliefs in human supremacy and difference from other animals, thus also carried the added burden of becoming a battleground for social theorists.

Herbert Spencer

Spencer is one of those not untypical products of nineteenth-century England. His family was not wealthy, but there was enough money for the young Spencer, originally trained as a railway engineer, to toy with the life of an inventor, then to settle into journalism, and finally to become a philosopher-science writer of very great influence in both Britain and the United States, and indeed to have had a significant impact on the likes of Ivan Pavlov in Russia. A utopian socialist and pacifist, Spencer came from a dissenting background and had a curious mix of beliefs. For example, committed to the notion of the greatest happiness for all, he believed the route to this was a profound individualism in which government's sole role is protection of the individual's rights to advancement but not the assistance and sustenance of the poor and indigent. They could go to the wall, and indeed Spencer saw this as a part of a "natural" process of social evolution which would eventually lead to better and happier people. By the 1850s Spencer had lost all religion, and had converted to a social naturalism and determinism based upon physiology and Lamarckian evolution.

In 1855 Spencer had published the first edition of his *Principles of Psychology*, the second edition of which in the 1870s is sometimes described as an exercise in evolutionary associationism. In a limited sense Spencer may be described as the first evolutionary psychologist. But his psychology, apart from its strong associationism borrowed from the sensationalists and a grudging acceptance of instincts in a fashion that Cabanis would have approved, bore little relation to modern psychology, or even to its earliest scientific forms. In brief, his psychology was a speculative exercise that had two main themes. The first was an associationism built around certain rules such as similarity of sensations, vividness, and repetition, which was wedded to one of his main conceptual principles of organization. This is the notion of "division of labor" and its embodiment physiologically and anatomically as an inexorable movement from a homogenous to an increasingly heterogeneous state, the principle deriving from the work of "real" physiologists and embryologists – Spencer read widely, if selectively. Thus the knowing human moves from a state of reflexive responses to the world to one of increasing knowledge gained through associative principles, and then to more integrated memory states and increasing rational capacity, though based always on the association of ideas.

The second theme is related in the sense that the same principle of movement along a scale from the simple and undifferentiated to the more complex and heterogeneous is appealed to; but now the scale is the grander one of species change within a Lamarckian framework. Species may be placed along a linear scale (here again is the *scala naturae*) from simple creatures to the more complex, in which complexity is manifested in both increasing division of labor of body parts and functions, and also psychological complexity where the scale moves from simple undifferentiated twitches and reflexes to more complex states of associative complexes, memory, and reasoning. Because Spencer was a convinced Lamarckian, the whole system of thought is based on a marriage of Lamarckian use and disuse and the inheritance of acquired characters to depict the evolution of mind as an inexorable movement in time from simple (like unicellular organisms) to complex species (like vertebrates), and from more lowly vertebrates (like fish) to more elevated vertebrates (such as mammals), and from humble mammals (insectivores, for instance) to the more elevated primates, and, of course, the scheme ends with humans – and then, and this is the big news – continues across specific human societies which change from "primitive" to "advanced" cultures.

Two specific points need to be made. The first is that Spencer was the first to make explicit the idea that learning by an individual might be incorporated into the characteristics of a species, that is, its instincts. Despite his sensationalist leanings, Spencer, like Cabanis before him, had to allow in instincts as inherited behavioral complexes because his Lamarckian stance forced him to it. Whether individual learning is or is not prior to the formation of species' instincts – which is just another formulation of the nature–nurture argument – figures large in subsequent developments of evolutionary ideas in psychology. The second point is that his introduction of these principles of progress via Lamarckian mechanisms into the evolution of individual human societies and cultures was the first naturalistic account of human culture. Spencer argued that the Lamarckian inheritance of "functionally produced modifications" is the chief cause of evolutionary change in human societies. The presumed ascent along some scale, which ended (of course) with white Europeans, was at once a "scientific" explanation of assumed racial supremacy, and a ray of hope for all human cultures because all, in time, would reach that supposedly exalted stage.

Spencer may be held these days to have been of little account. But that was not the case in Victorian England. He was a much admired figure, even by some of England's great minds like Darwin and John Stuart Mill, and a friend of the likes of Thomas Huxley. After Darwin's 1859 book had been published Spencer's evolutionary ideas, even though Lamarckian (though he did give way to some extent on the role of natural selection), received greater prominence. By the 1890s Lamarckian evolution was being seriously undermined by the work of August Weissmann, great German biologist and disciple of Darwin, and Spencer's influence began to wane a little. But not in the United States where Spencer's depiction of "survival of the fittest" (these were **not** words original to Darwin) and the extension of his ideas to human society enjoyed great vogue. Spencer was one of the parents of social Darwinism – even if his evolution was of a quite different sort to that of Darwin.

There is another reason why it is an error to relegate Spencer's role to that of minor importance. Social Darwinism, whether in Spencer's Lamarckian hands or in Francis Galton's Darwinian clutch (see next chapter), laid a claim to a biological takeover of the human sciences, with an accompanying down-playing of the forces of culture which are uniquely human. Culture became just another phenomenon to be understood and explained by wide-ranging biological principles. At the turn of the twentieth century it looked as if the biologists might win out in the explanation of what it means to be human. The founding of the science of genetics around 1900, and the rise in popularity of eugenics with its rallying cry of "nature not nurture" raised evolutionary theories of human cultural differences to such a pitch (see chapter 4) that finally, by around 1915, anthropologists felt compelled to cut themselves and their subject off from all biology, even while still nursing a grudging respect for Lamarck whose theory, as in Spencer's treatment, did not raise conceptually the barriers between peoples from different cultures in so impenetrable a way as did natural selection in the hands of Galton and his acolytes.

In this sense, then, Spencer bears partial responsibility for the driving out of biology from at least one of the emerging social sciences for many decades. But Spencer did damage in another, in a sense deeper, way. In running a Lamarckian story that notably fails to disambiguate individual experience from evolution, Spencer not only laid some of the foundations for the aggressive naturalization of the social sciences, he did this by running nature and nurture together in a single, seamless process and thus laid the foundation for endless confusion between the individual capacity for acquiring information (that is, learning in its many forms) and evolution. In an odd way, Spencer united nature and nurture, which we all now recognize is absolutely necessary, but because he did so in a way that was wrong, he did great damage. By running them together in an erroneous mix he stimulated efforts by social scientists to unmix and separate them entirely. But separating them is the beginning and end of a grave error – they **are** mixed and interdependent. They are **one thing,** when thought of in the right way. But proclaiming this wrongly, Spencer did great harm.

CHAPTER THREE

Psychology Born and the Darwinian Revolution

Lamarck's theory of evolution had generated much controversy but little science. Around the middle of the nineteenth-century evolutionary theory was recast in a different form, which has generated science aplenty ever since. At almost the same time, psychological science came into the world. Each was of considerable importance to how people would regard themselves. Had they been combined, their impact on Victorian thought would have been profound. Perhaps it was the reaction against the depth of that potential impact that resulted in their initial interaction being minimal. With the arrival of the twentieth century they drifted even further apart. That is the story of this chapter.

The New Science of Mind

Just as there can never be any certainty about the beginnings of human thought, so too are the lineages of any one idea of no clear origins. Every psychology student knows that the first psychology laboratory (well, it was just a small room, really) was established in Leipzig in 1879 by Wilhelm Wundt (1832–1920). But like evolutionary theory, a science of mind had been in the air for a very long time. The science of psychology does not suddenly begin in 1879. David Hume's mental mechanics with its association of ideas modeled along the lines of Newtonian physical mechanics was an early eighteenth-century precursor, Descartes' nerve spirits and mechanical models preceded Hume, as did Aristotle's *De Anima* long predate Descartes. A more recent precursor was the German astronomer Bessel who in 1816 read an account of an incident that had occurred at the Greenwich observatory some twenty years before when the Astronomer Royal, one Maskelyne, dismissed his assistant Kinnebrook because the latter persistently differed from his boss in estimating the times of stellar transits. This "error" on the part of his assistant, when projected onto the vastness of space, had significant consequences for the mapping of the universe, and would not do. Bessel was an expert in astronomical measurement with a strong interest in "errors." He began the systematic study of the time it takes to detect events, act on them, and (as in later work by the Dutch physiologist F.C. Donders) make decisions. He developed the notion of a "personal equation" for each observer which could then be corrected for in the stellar transit estimates of those individuals. What Bessel and Donders revealed was that mental work takes time, and time, of course, is both measurable and a common metric across all the natural sciences. Here, then, was a real basis for a natural science of mind. Such mental chronometry was appropriated by Wundt and others when a science of psychology was finally established as an empirical discipline; as studies in reaction time it became an absolutely standard methodology of twentieth-century laboratory psychology and remains so today. A few decades after Bessel's work the German physiologist Hermann von Helmholtz (1821-94) was able to measure the speed of conduction of the nerve impulse (which turned out to be much slower than previously thought). It began to make sense that mental events should have a measurable time dimension. Thus was laid the basis for marrying some future science of mind with the structure and function of the brain. The first psychology was bound to be a form of physiological psychology.

Equally important was the realization that, at least some, mental phenomena could be quantified and disciplined within mathematical formulae. Gustav Theodor Fechner (1801-87) trained in medicine and then later as a physicist; a subsequent personal crisis led to an interest in philosophy and hence to accounts of the human mind. He saw the importance of quantifying the processes of the mind and believed this could be achieved by relating bodily energy with the intensity of mental experience. Fechner knew of the work of Ernst Weber who was professor of anatomy and physiology at Leipzig University. Weber had previously demonstrated that the smallest perceptible difference between two sensations was a function of the ratio between the stimulus energies eliciting the sensations. For example, if for a stimulus of magnitude 50 an increase of 5 percent to 52.5 is necessary for a difference to be noted (52 or 51.5 not being judged as a different stimulus event), then if the original stimulus event is of a magnitude of 200 an increase in stimulus strength to 210 would be necessary for a difference to be detected. Fechner generalized Weber's finding to a law stating that the just noticeable differences between any pairs of stimuli in any sensory modality are perceptually equal which is then expressed in the mathematical form that the **perceived** magnitude of a stimulus is proportional to the logarithm of its **physical** intensity. Here again we have a link being established between mental events and measurable features of the natural world. In 1860 Fechner published a treatise called *Elemente der Psychophysik*. The very word psychophysics says it all. Potential conceptual bridges were being established between the physical world of things and aspects of the human mind, in this case, sensation. Much of this was happening around Leipzig where Wundt was later to establish his laboratory.

Wundt's life in science began as a physiologist. He studied with the great J. Muller who, despite his inability to shed somewhat mystical beliefs, trained an extraordinary number of Germany's, and other European states', most gifted physiologists. These included Helmholtz himself, as well as Virchow and du Bois-Reymond amongst scores of others. The period from about 1830 to 1860 was a wonderfully fertile one for German physiology, which came to stand as an example of how to practice good laboratory science. After a period as an assistant to Helmholtz, Wundt edged closer to his pioneering role by teaching a course on psychology as a natural science in 1862. Yet such is the difficulty of establishing the practice of a new science that it took a further 17 years before the conversion of that room in Leipzig into a psychology laboratory. It is worth pondering what was needed to achieve that.

Science is a form of knowledge of the world based on two closely intertwined processes. One is some kind of intellectual construction, usually in the form of causal explanation, as to the nature of that world, which in its highest form is theory. The other is observation of the world in as disciplined and careful a manner as possible to test the explanation. The theory guides the empiricism, and the findings of the latter corrects and molds the former. Nobody dissents from the view that scientific psychology was born out of a combination of philosophy and physiology. The philosophy provided the beginnings of theory, and the physiology gave the example of how to gather data to discipline the theory. Wundt's theory derived from his rationalism, what Thomas Leahey describes as a form of romantic German Platonism. He would have no truck with a reductive associationism modeled along the lines of Locke–Hume empiricism and sensationalism – no "tinker-toy model of the mind" (in Leahey's nice phrase) for him. The mainstay of Wundt's thinking centered on Leibniz's notion of apperception, which considered that the initial state of consciousness of any event is a kind of raw, undigested, perception which then becomes refined and sharpened into a clear conscious experience. In a sense, the orienting theory was the easy part of the problem. But what should your data be, and to how to collect it? It must be data *sui generis* which is unique enough to define the boundaries of the new discipline. Since psychology deals with the mind (Aristotle's *psyche*) and with apperception center-stage in his thinking, Wundt decided that the data was to be that deriving from immediate conscious experience by means of introspection, disciplined by the experimental methods borrowed from the likes of Bessel, Weber, and physiology at large.

One of his principle methods was subsequently adopted by psychologists of many different kinds and widely used throughout the twentieth century. This was to present for a brief period of time, in the region of a hundred milliseconds, some sensory input, usually visual, and then to ask the subject what they experienced. The input might be a set of abstract shapes, or unconnected letters, or letters which when combined made up a word or words. "What did you see?" the subject was asked. Meaning "what was in your mind during that brief moment?" Wundt, remember, was seeking to understand apperception and he quickly established that what is in conscious experience is determined not only by the elements of the sensory input, but also how they could be synthesized into large meaningful wholes under specific circumstances, and how factors such as attention and emotion enter as causes into consciousness. This may not sound ground breaking in the twenty-first century, but in the nineteenth century this was important news because he was gaining his data through experimentation of the like never attempted before. There were, however, serious problems which centered upon his exclusion of higher mental processes and, most importantly, on the use of introspection itself.

In the 1880s Hermann Ebbinghaus demonstrated that memory could be studied using a strict experimental methodology that, though refined, endured for a century. This showed that the new science of psychology need not be restricted to immediate conscious experience. Then one of Wundt's students, Oswald Kulpe, extended his method to the study of thought. He asked people to introspect on their thought processes whilst solving difficult problems. The results were a sensation. Some thoughts could be imaged and reported introspectively. Other thoughts occurred without conscious imagery at all. Reports of imageless thought (unconscious representations is perhaps a better phrase, George Mandler suggests) came from other parts of Europe using different methods. But, if some thought is imageless and hence cannot be introspected, why then the method is restricted at best, useless in studying important phenomena at worst. Wundt reacted by attacking sham, inadequately controlled experiments and the effects of fabrications based on the prior expectations of subjects. Well, perhaps. But what the whole episode revealed was that introspection is a thoroughly unreliable method. It also showed the importance of unconscious processing.

Parallel to his experimental psychology, often referred to as *Ganzheit* (which translates crudely as "holistic") psychology, Wundt in the latter part of his life wrote much on *Volkerpsychologie* (folk psychology). He considered that a full understanding of humans required that they be studied in the context of the language and customs of their cultures, which called for methods and analysis quite different from experimentation. This was psychology as traditions and history and was close to what was to become cultural anthropology. Whatever the failings of his experimental methods, Wundt's was a broad vision. His influence was immense, particularly in imbuing American scholars, who visited him or his disciples, with the understanding that the study of mind could be turned into a real natural science. Visitors, like William James, returned to the United States and spread the message that while the method of introspection might be wrong, the vision of such a science was not. By the turn of the twentieth century, the center of gravity of psychological science had shifted across the Atlantic. Europe would continue to produce great psychologists, like Piaget and Pavlov and Bartlett, but the engine driving the discipline became firmly anchored in North America.

At about the time that psychological science began its substantial move from Europe to America, Sigmund Freud (1856–1939) was developing a dynamic theory of the human mind in which unconscious mental processes were postulated as central. Freud's theory was essentially one of a structured mind in which instincts and developmental experience figured large. No psychological theory has had a greater cultural impact than that of Freud. As science though it has always been controversial. If introspection of conscious experience was judged unreliable, how much more suspect are interpretations of the unconscious mind by someone standing outside of that mind. Here was a realm which was widely judged to be beyond empirical science. No one now doubts that there are processes of mind that are unconscious (we all employ them each time we effortlessly rise from bed or articulate a sentence in our native language) but whether they are of the kind that Freud claimed is a quite different matter. Nonetheless, Freud was an instinct theorist, and as such was greatly interested in evolutionary theory. As a young man Freud had carried out fundamental physiological research in fish and he interpreted his results in terms of what Darwin in *Descent* referred to as "arrests of development." In his *Introductory Lectures on Psycho-Analysis* Freud was to develop this idea in terms of "fixation . . . of the instinct." He was directly applying a Darwinian "mechanism" to his theory. The same interest in and application of evolutionary theory cannot be said of Wundt and the other early physiological psychologists. Fechner, Wundt, and the likes of Helmholz were knowledgeable people. They knew about Lamarck and by the 1860s were aware of Darwinian theory. However, their thoughts and experiments owed not a jot to evolutionary theory of any kind. Wundt, in fact, was a Lamarckian, and when Weismann effectively killed off that version of evolutionary theory in the 1880s, at least to the satisfaction of biologists, Wundt lost interest in evolutionary biology.

The Darwinian Revolution

Charles Darwin (1809–1882) conceived a theory of evolution very different from that of Lamarck. Contrary to the cant of creationists and other less inspired critics, evolution is not a monolithic theory. It has changed repeatedly over the last two hundred years in response to new findings and novel ideas, and doubtless will change again in the future. But, roughly speaking, the theory in its various forms conforms to two broad types, of which the Lamarckian and Darwinian are archetypal versions. For Lamarck evolution is driven wholly by external forces of change which, mediated by the altered needs and activities of organisms, become **impressed** by these external changes upon the malleable substrate of the organism and then transmitted to offspring. This is an instructionist theory of transformation. The changes in the world precede and cause the changes in life forms. Darwin's theory, in contrast, was selectionist. Organisms, he argued, occur in innumerable variant forms. These differences, variation, are caused by events internal to each organism and occur in advance of and unconnected with changes in the world. Selection, natural selection as Darwin called it, is the process by which some of these undirected (sometimes misleadingly called "blind") changes are incorporated into an integrated bodily structure and function better suited to survival and reproductive competence (fitness), and somehow transmitted to offspring. For Darwin, evolution is driven by selectionist processes in contrast to Lamarck's instructionist paradigm. For Darwin, changes in organisms occur prior to, and independent of, the events in the world but then may become permanently incorporated into the lineage of an organism insofar as these features, adaptations, are heritable and furnish the organisms with increases in fitness.

There is another fundamental difference between these two forms of evolutionary theory. For Lamarck, remember, a linear scale (the *scala naturae*) represented evolution as a series of transformations leading to life's ascent; for Darwin, evolution is change as descent from some original life form via a complex tree structure with contemporary species representing the current end points of the myriad branches. In his notebooks, Darwin reminded himself never to refer to species as "lower" or "higher" than others. They are just different from one another, but always related, no matter how remotely. It should be said that what is presented here is an idealized form of Darwin's theory. *The Origin of Species*, first published in 1859, appeared in six editions, and in later ones Darwin began to incorporate elements of Lamarckian theory into his own, especially some kind of inheritance of acquired characteristics. Partly this was a result of his not having any idea, nor did anyone else, of the origins of variation or the means of transmission between parents and offspring. Partly it was because the physicist Kelvin was casting doubt upon the depth of geological time and Darwin needed a way of speeding up evolution. However, absolutely central to his theory was natural selection, and the Darwinian scheme is often depicted as a process theory (i.e. he proposed no mechanisms but put forward what it was the mechanisms, whatever they are, are causing) of three parts: there is the generation of variants, the selection of some small number of these, and their transmission to offspring and hence their propagation into the future.

Variation, selection, and transmission (heritability). In time the endless repetition of what we would now call this evolutionary algorithm through thousands of millions of years (Kelvin was wrong and the geologists right) results in the formation of new species characterized by specific arrays of adaptations to the niches that they occupy, and the selection pressures that the niches exert.

Thus it is that Mayr asserted that Darwin had solved the problem of teleology. When a turtle swims ashore and lays its eggs we can properly say that it swam ashore in order to lays its eggs, not because the individual turtle has conscious intentional agency and not because the turtle has *a priori* knowledge about sandy beaches and egg-laying, but because eons of selection acting *a posteriori* upon variant egg-laying behaviors had resulted in a particular species-typical behavior as an adaptation for laying eggs. Here we have Aristotelian final cause turned into science with what appears to be *a priori* knowledge explained by the *a posteriori* explanation of descent with modification. This example makes a further point. When people think of adaptations they are inclined to envisage the wonders of the vertebrate eye or the intricacies of the workings of single cells. But Darwin devoted an entire chapter of the 1859 book to instinct, which he defined thus:

> An action, which we ourselves require experience to enable us to perform, when performed by an animal, more especially by a very young one, without experience, and when performed by many individuals in the same way, without their knowing for what purpose it is performed, is usually said to be instinctive. (In Mentor, 1958, p. 228)

Furthermore, said Darwin:

> instincts are as important as corporeal structures for the welfare of each species, under its present conditions of life. Under changed conditions of life, it is at least possible that slight modifications of instinct might be profitable to a species; and if it can be shown that instincts do vary ever so little, then I can see no difficulty in natural selection preserving and continually accumulating variations of instinct to any extent that was profitable. It is thus, as I believe, that all the most complex and wonderful instincts have originated. (In Mentor edition, 1958, p. 229)

For Darwin instincts were on the agenda of evolutionary theory. What applies to organismic structure applies just as well to behaviors that fall within his definition of instinct. As to whether evolution applies to humans he was famously reticent in the original edition of the 1859 book. In later editions he was less guarded:

> In the future I see open fields for far more important researches. Psychology will be securely based on the foundation already well laid by Mr. Herbert Spencer, that of the necessary acquirement of each mental power and capacity by gradation. Much light will be thrown on the origin of man and his history. (In Mentor edition, 1958, p. 449)

Even less guarded was he in *The Descent of Man and Selection in Relation to Sex* which was published in 1871. In this work Darwin devoted two chapters to a comparison of the mental powers of ourselves and "lower" animals (thus violating his injunction to himself to avoid using such words). Diverse topics were surveyed, ranging from memory and imitation to tool use, language, a sense of beauty, morals, and conscience. The evidence given to support his argument which aims "to shew that there is no fundamental difference between man and the higher mammals in their mental faculties" is a catalog of outrageous anecdotes gained from his correspondence with a wide variety of people located in different parts of the globe. Drunken baboons who, on the morning after "held their aching heads ... and wore a most pitiable expression" are described along with monkeys that learn to open eggs in such a way as not to lose their contents on the ground, and dogs drawing sledges who spread their positions relative to one another when encountering thin ice and thus reducing the pressure of their combined weight and lessening the likelihood of plunging through to icy water. By modern standards of animal behavior studies, indeed as will be seen, by the standards that began to be observed just a few decades later, no credence at all can be given to this evidence. Most of it was probably totally unreliable, and what little may seem credible might carry quite different interpretations to those Darwin placed on them.

Such dubious behavioral evidence apart, Darwin's arguments were almost always cogent. But in one respect he was unusually uncertain and contradictory. This concerned the relationship between instinct and intelligence. Did intelligent creatures like apes have more or less instincts than less intelligent animals? He offered both possibilities within pages of one another and couldn't settle on a fixed position. The related question of just how intelligent behaviors are related to those that are instinctive was also unresolved. Both issues were later to be developed in significant ways by others.

The thrust of his arguments in the early chapters of *Descent* was an attack on the position that we are of unique intelligence. We are not, he was asserting, the epistemological wonders that we like to think we are. The second half of the book he devoted to sexual selection, which broadly speaking is the idea that some heritable traits are selected for, not because of their contribution to overall fitness, but because they enhance the chances of reproductive success. The point he was making was that he saw communality of forces acting on both *Homo sapiens* and other species that reproduce sexually. A couple of years later he published a book in which he argued that in the expression of emotions we are also no different from related species.

In contrast with his earlier reticence, when he likened talking about evolution in public as being like confessing to a murder, Darwin came clean in the 1870s. The sweep of his claims was wide. Neither man nor other creatures are the result of divine creation. We are all products of the same natural laws, and man is just another animal, albeit an interesting one. The cogency of his argument, and the evidence on which it was based, that made the 1859 book so powerful was to some extent reduced by the weakness of the evidence he adduced for the behavior of man and, especially, other animals, in his later work. It was, though, to be a significant legacy.

Darwin's Immediate Successors

Darwin's genius is not in doubt. But it is precisely because of his towering achievements that it is easy to overstate his contribution to evolutionary biology. When he died we had a theory much superior to anything that had come before, and through that a new way of understanding the distribution of living things in time and space, a powerful account of the natural design of adaptations, and the notion of common descent as an explanation of similarity and dissimilarity of traits between members of different species. But evolutionary biology did not spring fully formed from Darwin. The work of Mendel, the father of genetics, remained unknown until 20 years after Darwin's death. It was well into the twentieth century before geneticists were able to provide evolutionary theory with some of the mechanisms that drive Darwin's processes of transformation. Darwin and his disciples knew nothing of such developments, of course, and many took seriously the (soon to be discredited) Lamarckian ideas on the effects of use and disuse and their inheritance. The precise ways in which speciation occurs were not known. Indeed so much was then unknown, including the pace of evolutionary change. Darwin insisted on its being slow and gradual. His great defender, Thomas Huxley, was doubtful on this score, but few others were at that time and so no one expected literally to see evolutionary change occurring and the widespread assumption was that the evidence to support the theory would always be indirect. One hunderd and forty years on, we now have observed instances of evolution and a mass and precision of information that would have amazed and delighted Darwin.

The principle of specific application stated in chapter 1, which avers that evolution only enters into psychology to the extent that specific features of the theory drive both empirical studies and the explanations of their findings, leads us to expect that the initial application of evolution to studies of mind would be as vague and ill-formed as the state of evolutionary biology was in the late nineteenth century. If evolution was to enter into psychology, it would have to be by way of the comparison of the minds of animals and humans based upon the notion of continuity of some kind between humans and other animals. But the comparative method, in the light of the new theory of evolution, was itself not yet well formed at that time, and the phrase "continuity between species" was wracked with uncertainty. How much continuity? And just what did continuity mean and what expectations did it create? If species A is nine tenths like species B (even if this could be measured then, and it could not), would this mean that the minds, the psychological processes and mechanisms (had these been known at the time, and they were not) of species A would likewise be nine tenths like species B? It was all so uncertain and tentative. Psychology itself was in its infancy, and so all that people had were vague ideas, what now would be called folk psychology, about the animal minds driving the behaviors that were observed in a haphazard and unreliable fashion. The results were not surprising.

For Huxley we were conscious automata and in this Cartesian sense, no different from other animals. But the person to carry Darwin's flag forward in the study of minds was not Huxley but George Romanes (1848–94) who took an almost opposite view. For Romanes the important belief was that animals can make choices, and this can be seen in the way they behave. Specifically, Romanes reasoned that it was choice based upon past experience that mattered, and that meant the capacity for learning.

Often described as Darwin's heir, if in fact Darwin thought of him in that light it was because his late years saw an increasing interest in the application of his theory to humans, and specifically our minds, Romanes had begun as a physiologist with a strong religious belief. He came to Darwin's work in the 1870s and it had a profound effect on him. The religion drained away from him but not the interest in things spiritual in the broad sense, hence his focus on the evolution of mind, and that meant understanding the minds of animals. Like his mentor, he began to collect stories about the behavior of animals, made observations of his own, and even housed a monkey with his sister. Despite the huge influence of Darwin on him, Romanes, like Spencer, who he much admired, was a Lamarkian. Indeed his general conceptual stance was very close to Spencer. Instincts were not viewed as unmodifiable by experience, and habit, he argued, could in some species be the precursor of instinct.

Three books were the products of Romanes' labors. They contained numerous anecdotes, often as outrageous as Darwin's – indeed Darwin was sometimes his source – and a considerable amount of theory which serves as a signpost to later developments in both psychology and, some decades later, ethology. As Robert Boakes notes, Romanes lapsed into a Lamarckian progressivism in which animal minds were depicted as evolving **towards** human intelligence. This was a most un-Darwinian stance and, in the end, no kind of scientific contribution at all. And despite his grounding in physiology, Romanes conducted no controlled experiments either. Yet he stands as a key link in the story of evolutionary thinking about the mind, human or otherwise, because of his relationship to Conway Lloyd Morgan (1852–1936) who was a highly significant figure.

Although just a few years younger than Romanes, Morgan's contributions came later in his life than did those of Romanes, and so a kind of succession in their rank and thinking is evident. Morgan was deeply skeptical about, and critical of, the anecdotal "method" and, with the exception of Douglas Spalding, a young English naturalist of some 20 years earlier, may be considered the first comparative psychologist to use experiments. They may not have been the kinds of controlled and systematic studies that experimental psychologists routinely began to use through much of the twentieth century, but they nonetheless provided Morgan with a more secure base on which to develop his ideas. Observing the behavioral development of chicks with care, inserting changes into their environments and recording the effects (hence the experimental method), and playing games with his dog but in most constructive ways, Morgan came to two broad conclusions. The first was that the Darwin–Romanes conclusions as to the lofty intellectual abilities of nonhuman animals was largely anthropomorphic nonsense. Romanes' sister's monkey may, and only may, have used a screw-like device **as if** it understood the principle of the screw, but that merely indicated an appropriate action, not an understanding. Second, this did not mean Morgan thought animals were conscious automata. He had no time for quasi-philosophical speculations about consciousness in other species, but he certainly did not think them automata. On the basis of the animals he was looking at, and no matter that this was a very limited number (the usual suspects were chicks, dogs, cats, monkeys, and apes), their behavior showed a flexibility that could derive only from learning.

Morgan, over a highly fruitful period of about twenty years, showed just how the discipline should advance. Although a Lamarckian early in his career he soon corrected that error and became a hard-nosed Darwinian. Unlike many later comparative psychologists, an evolutionary foundation to all his thoughts was constant. On the other hand, he was at once cautious and perspicacious in the relative roles he assigned to evolution and individual learning. Morgan was the first to understand that here was a delicate balancing act by nature which had nothing to do with the inheritance of acquired characters. Both evolution and individual learning were the causes of the behavior of the animals he was observing, but just how much causal force to assign to each? This is, this was, and this always will be one of the key questions to be solved by evolutionary psychology (see chapters 6 and 7). Morgan understood its importance and his answer was a surprisingly modern one. He understood that "experience carries on from the results of evolution," as Boakes puts it, and for Morgan the results of evolution need only be minimal. He believed that certain limited, if key, parts of the wiring of the brains of animals are innate (i.e. genetically part-determined in modern parlance), namely emotional responses to certain classes of events and the organization of coherent actions as responses to such events, and that attaching to these are some relatively simple learning processes that are able to associate consistently linked features of the world (in effect, the detection and conservation of cause–effect relations in the world, though Morgan would not have used such terms). The learning processes would act as a means of scaffolding a small number of innate behaviors to result in a rich repertoire of adaptive behaviors. This is a very "modern" stance, closely similar to what in chapter 7 is referred to as a developmental empiricist position. Minimal innate traits, a general learning process, and a reliable species-typical developmental environment and you have a highly effective means of generating complex and effective behavior. Complex problem solving and the ability for abstract reasoning are not required. Morgan's canon, that one should not "interpret an action as the outcome of the exercise of a higher psychical faculty, if it can be interpreted as the outcome of the exercise of one which stands lower in the psychological scale" is a famous criticism of the Victorian penchant for assigning higher psychical faculties to birds, bees, and baboons. It was a powerful put down of Darwin and Romanes and it had an evolutionary logic. Why would complex costly processes evolve if simpler and cheaper ones could do the job?

Morgan made a number of other seminal contributions. He anticipated a possible distinction that was subsequently to become absolutely fundamental to twentieth-century learning theory. This is that learning to associate sensory inputs is different from learning to associate a behavior with its consequences. He was remarkably insightful about how songbirds acquire their song, an issue that a later chapter will explain was not trivial in its implications. He understood the importance of imitation and like Alfred Russell Wallace, he was skeptical about the role of evolution in explaining the minds of modern humans. He believed that as a social animal without peer, humans are what they are in the present because culture had taken over where evolution had left off. He also argued for what now would be considered a form of memetics, and was a strong advocate, perhaps the original, of organic selection, both of which will be explained in subsequent chapters.

Morgan is simply one of the most important people in this history because, in the rigor of his analyses, he was able to anticipate all of the major questions confronting the general problem of how to get evolution into psychology. Morgan gets little historical recognition now, which cannot be said for Darwin's cousin, Francis Galton (1822–1911), whose fame rests not on any contribution to this or any other science, but on his making serious trouble for the naturalization of the social sciences.

Darwin was not convinced that human intelligence would evolve beyond what it was in modern humans. He thought there was insufficient variation for selection to act on. His cousin disagreed. Galton certainly had some outstanding features for a Victorian biologist. He was passionate about the necessity for quantitative measurement, declaring that if you can't measure it then it isn't science. Famously he compared the life spans of those much prayed for (members of royal families and senior figures in the churches) with other elevated members of society (lawyers and others in the British gentry) and found them no different. He concluded that there was no efficacy in prayer. The development of statistical concepts and measurement, like correlation and regression, either by himself or by his disciples like Karl Pearson were to become some of psychology's most important tools. These were real and lasting contributions. He also dabbled in experiments on memory, introducing the use of word association tests. But what Galton is best known for is his constant advocacy of the hereditary basis of almost all aspects of the human mind, ranging from differences in sensory acuity to moral judgment. Galton read his cousin's first book and was instantly converted to a staunch evolutionism. Like almost everyone else of that period he played at times with Lamarckian notions but needed little persuasion by the work of Weismann or the writings of others to believe that natural selection acted on hereditary factors. The title of his first book, *Hereditary Genius,* says it all. Everything else that he wrote was a repetition or variation on that theme. He collected data on family lineages and their achievements, good or bad; he established the methodology of studying twins; and he used questionnaires to generate data on peoples' attitudes. Surprisingly, he never developed any tests of intelligence, which was to become a thriving industry in twentieth-century psychology, his data was of doubtful quality, and he was hopelessly biased in his analyses of what data he had. Without any understanding of the force of culture and individual experience, and so contrary to the ideas of the likes of Wallace and Morgan, Galton laid almost all cause for psychological characteristics at the feet of what was to become genetics. Darwin himself disagreed with him but to no avail.

This would have made of him no more than a zealot for hereditary explanations were it not tied to Galton's bigotry regarding women, "lower" classes, and other races, and the association of his prejudices with evolutionary theory. The result was a biological theory of racial differences and his fervent preaching of humankind's salvation lying in allowing only selected breeding between peoples of favored characteristics – and what was favored was determined by Galton's racism. In 1883 Galton first introduced the term "eugenics." He had by then polarized explanations of the human mind into Shakespeare's nature or nurture (in *The Tempest* Prospero describes Caliban as "a devil, a born devil, on whose nature Nurture can never stick") and considered nature to have many times the causal force of nurture in making us what we are. And he strenuously advocated a prohibition on the having of children by those he considered feckless, idle, or evil.

There is an odd paradox here. Galton's fears for the future of humanity rest on the assumption that we are possessed of, or have created, something, culture, which is of a sufficiently great force to shield our species from the effects of natural selection. He believed that because of this natural selection was somehow failing to exert the influence that it should, and so people with undesirable traits, like criminality or stupidity, bred unchecked and threatened the future of *Homo sapiens*. In effect he believed that nurture was winning out over nature, the polarization of causes that he himself had forced, despite his having crassly and spuriously quantified nature as being overwhelmingly greater in causal power. He seemed never to realize that his stance was thus riddled by contradiction.

Early in the twentieth century, eugenics was starting to appear as academically respectable. Pearson was on the staff of University College London and Galton was instrumental in funding the salaries of people working in the cause of eugenics within that institution. By then eugenics had also crossed the Atlantic and was a rising movement in the United States. Galton was culpable on two counts. The first is conceptual in that, in contrast to Morgan, he had cleaved nature and nurture apart again, thus playing into the hands of those whose agenda was opposite to that of Galton himself; fanatical environmentalists could champion nurture because the hereditareans like Galton had insisted that their own intellectual money was on nature, and they could do so because Galton had asserted they are different things. The second is that eugenics outraged and frightened many people, not least those working in the new social sciences. Galton was a massive obstacle in the way of forging links between the human and natural sciences.

Early Psychology in the United States

After the ending of the Civil War, the United States began to undergo massive change. Industrialization occurred on a huge scale, and there were unprecedented population shifts away from the countryside with the creation of ever larger urban conurbations. In the twenty years leading to 1900 the population of American cities almost doubled. As a result the educational system had to respond to the needs of new technological demands on a relatively undereducated population. New universities began to be established on a scale never seen before, and these were innovative in the introduction of novel degree programs suited to the needs of a country transforming itself. The new universities became the centers of science, with a new form of academic – someone who both taught and practiced science. This was without precedent, and it revolutionized the influence of people working in universities. It was within this framework that the new science of psychology became established in a manner that was not to occur in Europe for decades. Indeed, that a science of mind could be harnessed to the needs of a country was an idea that America adopted when no other country did. For these reasons psychology since the early twentieth century became preeminently an American science.

Leahey records how in 1871 a small group of young Bostonians called the Metaphysical Club began to meet regularly. Among them was Charles Peirce and William James, under whose influence psychology was to shift decisively away from the structuralism of European psychology with its emphasis on the content of consciousness, towards a pragmatism and functionalism in which what mattered was not what is **in** consciousness, but what it is **for** and how it works. James (1842–1910) was seminal in this transformation. Never a practicing psychologist, James was a philosopher who knew his physiology and understood physiological psychology from his frequent travels in Europe. He was the first teacher of the subject in America and used Spencer's book as his text. At that time Spencer was all the rage in north America. His progressive evolutionism combined with slogans like "survival of the fittest" had made of him every person's favorite philosopher – this, after all, was the land of the free where anyone could rise to anything in a society and where free enterprise ran riot. But James was not happy with Spencer, who, remember, was an unreconstructed Lamarckian, and Lamarck's evolution was one that applied to passive living forms responding slavishly to the changes forced on them by changes in the world. James wanted a psychology based on active individuals who are products of Darwinian evolution. James eventually wrote his own two-volume *Principles of Psychology* that was to replace Spencer's and shape all twentieth-century psychology. The contrast between Spencer's *Principles* and that of James is stark. Spencer's work actually contains little that would be recognized as psychology today, whereas James' looks, in subject matter, like almost any modern introductory text. James was firmly materialistic, with habits depicted as new "pathways through the nerve-centers" and "the enormous flywheel of society" (an interesting anticipation of what was to become the ideational school of culture – culture as acquired knowledge). Habit aside, his chapter headings included instinct, attention, stream of consciousness (very different from Wundt's static view), the self, reasoning, and will amongst others. All was grounded in Darwinian theory. For instance early in volume one he wrote that "mind and world...have been evolved together, and in consequence are something of a mutual fit"; and "mental life is primarily teleological" by which he meant that how we think and feel are "because of their utility in shaping our *reactions* on the outer world" (italics in the original showing James' emphasis on the pragmatics of psychology); and consciousness "has in all probability been evolved, like all other functions, for a use."

Well, from this it would seem that evolution was alive and well in early twentieth-century American psychology because James' influence was huge then. But this is not so. True, James was a stalwart Darwinian. It was a starting premise for him. But unlike Morgan or Romanes, there was no principle of specific application in his theory. For Romanes, remember, the specific application was in terms of continuity between species, no matter how vague the notion of continuity was; for Morgan it was the role of individual learning in the development of adaptive behaviors; but for James it was a background commitment to the vague notion that things had to have some kind of functional (survival or reproductive) value. Things of the mind **worked**, because they were the products of evolution, but the pragmatics and functionalism were not honed into specific analytical tools within psychological theory, neither by James himself, nor by those he influenced like John Dewey and James Angell and other members of the Chicago functionalist school (circa 1890–1910) who in turn had significant effects on the thinking of a new generation of psychologists.

Descartes' reflexology was then being resurrected in modern form by new physiological understanding of the reflex arc which was seen to be the basic functional unit of nervous system activity translated into observable behavior. At the same time, in Russia I.P. Pavlov was discovering the conditioned reflex and laying the experimental foundation for understanding conditioning as a fundamental form of associative learning. The reflex, conditioned or unconditioned, as a **functional** unit laid stress on how things worked, but this is semantically a long way from the **functionalism** that links to adaptive utility. The words function and functional share the same root, of course, but they are worlds apart semantically. If evolution was to maintain a presence in psychology in the first part of the twentieth century it was either as a pun deriving from the confusion of "why" and "how" (Boring confuses things further by quoting from Angell that functional psychology is the "psychology of mental operations in contrast to the psychology of mental elements"), or as a vague background assumption. It is easy to find in the writings of virtually every important psychologist of the last one hundred years instances of the latter. For example, in 1943, Clark L. Hull, then a learning theorist of enormous influence wrote in his *Principles of Behavior* that "the processes of organic evolution have produced a nervous system in the higher organisms which" elicits behaviors that terminate needs without learning; and in 1953, B.F. Skinner, an even more important figure in twentieth-century psychology, in *Science and Human Behavior* asserted that "Reflexes and other innate patterns of behavior evolve because they increase the chances of survival of the species." But in neither case is the theory of evolution actually used either to develop a theoretical position by specific application or to direct specific empirical studies. It is a form of hand-waving, and important as James and Dewey were, it was a waving of hands that began with them. If evolution had any presence in psychology at the start of the twentieth century, it was as a kind of ghost, a presence without any substance. Soon even the ghost was to be exorcized.

CHAPTER FOUR

The Near Death of Darwinism in the Social Sciences

Not long after Darwin died his theory nearly followed him into oblivion. Then a synthesis between the concept of natural selection and genetics occurred, and by 1959, the centenary year of the publication of *The Origin of Species*, what had become known as the modern synthesis, or neo-Darwinism, appeared to be a robust and scientifically unchallenged theory. One of its twentieth-century luminaries, Theodosius Dobzhansky, declared that nothing in biology makes sense except in the light of evolution. Whatever the truth of that assertion, within the social sciences, which are those sciences concerned with what makes humans different from other species, evolutionary theory withered and all but disappeared in the period from around 1915 for some 50 years. Whilst evolutionary theory is not directly our subject, its application within psychology is, and that application cannot be separated from developments in the theory itself. So first it is those developments up to 1959 that will be briefly outlined. Then the stalling of the process of conceptually marrying the social sciences with other natural sciences, notably evolutionary biology, will be considered.

Evolution after Darwin

Darwin had some great champions in Germany. One was August Weismann (1834–1914). He actually tested, albeit very badly, the belief that acquired traits could be inherited and found it to be false. His principal contribution, the doctrine of the separation of the germ (sex) cells from body (soma) cells, embodied his conviction that there is simply no means by which changes in the soma could induce alterations in germ cells. Weismann became a powerful advocate for natural selection as being one of the principal forces driving evolution and proponent-in-chief for the abolition of all forms of Lamarckian theory. His influence was considerable and it was he more than anyone else who was responsible for the gradual purging of Lamarckism from biology. With the exception of the advocates of Lysenkoism in the Soviet Union who represented a grotesque return to Lamarckian ideas in a vain attempt to match genetics to ideology, Lamarckism in its original form gradually disappeared. There have been tiny flurries of excitement every so often, most recently in the 1980s, with reports, always wrong, that evidence has been found for directed evolution and the inheritance of acquired characters. As long as the inheritance is by way of what Weismann called the germ plasm (sex cells or gametes in modern parlance), it is reasonable to conclude that Lamarckian evolution is truly dead.

The "continuity of the germ plasm," Weismann's doctrine, became one of the main foundations of modern biology. But though as hard-nosed a Darwinian as one could get, Weismann understood that evolutionary theory stood in dire need of a proper science of inheritance. Because of a visual disability Weismann was no experimenter, and it would take the work of someone else to establish that science. That someone else was an obscure Moravian monk, Gregor Mendel, the discovery of whose work (by a number of people independently leading some to believe a conspiracy had been in place to hide the missing pieces of the puzzle) marks the beginning of what is arguably the most successful of all twentieth-century science, genetics.

Mendel's is an odd story. He had wanted to be a schoolteacher and spent a year at the University of Vienna having been sponsored by the monastery at Brno. But his teachers there found him wanting and after just one year he was sent back to the monastery. No teaching for him. Given what he was to achieve, we may be forgiven for revising the judgment as to who was wanting in the case. Born on a farm and so with a background in folk botany, but with an intense interest in plants and biology in general (he was later to read Darwin), back at the monastery he began a series of experiments on varieties of edible peas. The consensus of geneticists is that he was either extraordinarily lucky or very clever. He was certainly very original because what he did was cross-breed different strains of pea (differing in color of flower, size of plant, form of pea, and so on) and sorted the offspring according to which of the parental traits the offspring showed, and **counted them**, thus deriving mathematical ratios. This had never been done before. Contrary to the prevailing views of genetics of the time which was some form of blending, what Mendel found was that particular characteristics (like a color of flower) might disappear from one generation, but then reappear in a later generation with their integrity maintained even if not always expressed in an individual. Bronowski points out that it beggars belief that blending could ever have been a serious genetic idea because it had always been known that the union of man and woman results always in a child who grows to be one or the other and not something intermediate, though traits like size, which are controlled by many genes, might have confused the issue. In any event, Mendel provided definitive proof that blending is simply a wrong conception. Most importantly, he showed that the appearance of traits across different filial generations occurs in specific ratios (3:1 often, sometime 9:3:3:1 in dihybrid crosses for instance), and from these ratios he drew specific inferences. One was that phenotypic traits are transmitted from parents to offspring by specific "factors," which later came to be called genes. Another was that these factors occurred in variant forms which give rise to variant traits (like different colors, or sizes). A third was that these variant forms are either dominant or recessive in expression.

These were magnificent data and impeccable inferences. Mendel published them in the *Journal of the Brno Natural History Society*, which while not quite the equivalent of the *South Wessex Organic Gardeners' Annual Report* of today, was not a route to fame. He did communicate with a biologist of some repute, Nageli, but Nageli was totally committed to the notion of blending inheritance and seemed simply to misunderstand the significance of Mendel's work. Mendel was snubbed insofar as he made any contact at all with the world of science. He was not snubbed by his fellow monks. In 1868 he was made abbot of his monastery. By 1871 he had ceased all breeding experiments, and following his death in 1884 his successor burnt all his papers. It is reasonably certain that Darwin knew nothing of his work.

The single great contribution Mendel made was that inheritance is particulate and that the factors contributed by both parents do not fuse in the offspring but are somehow separated out again during the formation of gametes and transmitted intact to the offspring of the offspring. Here was proof positive of Weismann's doctrine. And here were the foundations of a proper science of inheritance. From Mendel's data two laws were derived (the law of segregation and the law of independent assortment) that became the mainstay of genetics in the early years of the twentieth century. The co- but independent discoverers of Mendel's studies (de Vries, Correns, and Tschermak) were already generating their own data and the emergence of a vibrant science quickly replicated and extended Mendel's work. The basis for sudden changes in characters, mutations, was established and all this was supplemented by cytological findings that located genes on chromosomes within the nuclei of cells, and which began to map events in the nucleus of the cell when they divide to form near identical somatic daughter cells (mitosis) or when gametes are formed (meiosis). Gene linkage, chromosomal cross-overs and gene-gene (epistatic) interactions were discovered and studied in minute detail. One of the most glaring implications was that sexual reproduction is a device that generates variation on a truly astronomical scale. One of Darwin's old headaches was cured. Here was a source of massive and continuous variation.

However, what seemed to answer one problem for evolution led to the creation of another. If genetics could reveal the sources of flux and change in populations of organisms, what need was there for the notion of evolution via natural selection? If genes spontaneously mutated, and if such genes were crucial in the formation of key traits, or if multiple mutations arose in concert to give rise to macromutations, these might be the source of speciation. The small and gradual changes that Darwin postulated were thought to be irrelevant. Natural selection was widely deemed irrelevant by the likes of de Vries and Bateson, leaders of the new science, who opposed the idea, not of evolution, but of natural selection as a causal force in that process.

The problem was one of reconciling the continuous variation in natural populations that biometricians were reporting with the particulate notion of genes coming from the laboratories of the geneticists. In 1918 an English biologist, R.A. Fisher (1890–1962), wrote a seminal paper that did just that. This was then followed by a series of classic papers and books by Fisher, J.B.S. Haldane (1892–1964), another Englishman, and the American Sewall Wright (1889–1988), all of which wedded Darwin's natural selection process with Mendelian genetics. All showed persuasively that evolution could occur if selection operated on natural variation that followed the laws of Mendelian genetics. Neither the inheritance of acquired characters, by then repeatedly shown not to occur in any event, nor directed variation, nor macromutations were necessary. What was more, these new approaches, which later came to be called the modern synthesis, were captured within mathematical formulations. Subsequent developments involved changing conceptions of just how to characterize species, the circumstances under which speciation occurs, in which Mayr was a central figure, and the demonstration by George Gaylord Simpson and others of the consistency of the modern synthesis with the palaeontological record.

There were differences of opinion and approach, of course. One interesting conceptualization of evolution involved fitness landscapes with peaks and troughs of adaptiveness for different species or populations. Climbing up to one peak of fitness might leave a species stranded and unable to bridge the troughs that separate it from even higher fitness peaks. How might species negotiate the difficulties presented by such theoretical landscapes? Indeed how could adaptations in the same organism accommodate to separate landscapes for each adaptation? These were difficult questions. Fisher inclined to favor the efficacy of small mutations over those having large effects, developing a proof for larger mutations having correspondingly smaller results in climbing fitness peaks. Sewell Wright, by contrast, favored the role of random genetic drift.

Such disputes aside, by the 1950s evolutionary theory seemed firmly based on natural selection acting on random mutation, recombination, and drift, with gene flows between populations combining with geographical features to give rise to changes in gene frequencies supporting organisms adaptively fit to survive and reproduce in particular environments. Speciation was the product of such events which, if carried on over long enough periods would give rise to higher taxonomic levels. The succession of natural selection pressures in history had been married to increasingly well-understood mechanisms. In 1953 a paper authored by J. Watson and F. Crick appeared in the journal *Nature* which offered an understanding of genes in terms of the double helix structure of deoxyribonucleic acid (DNA). The era of molecular biology had begun and it seemed then that evolutionary theory and evolutionary biology had indeed come of age.

Behaviorism Takes Hold in Psychology

As noted in the previous chapter, evolutionary theory had but a ghostly presence in early American psychology, and, the damaging Galton and his followers apart, very little in that of Europe. Labeled "functionalism," it was a long way removed from any specific conception of evolution or adaptation. It centered on the vague notion that what is fundamental to a scientific psychology is adjustment to change. Nothing stands still. Nothing remains the same. Unlike the fixed laws of Newton and the supposedly immutable structures of chemistry proposed by Mendeleev, Darwin's theory was premonitory of a broad swathe of twentieth-century science in which flux and change are writ large. If species had not been of a fixed form for all of time, why should this not apply also to the chemical elements and the stars in the heavens? In 1900 nobody explicitly articulated the centrality of transformation to the science of the new century and even now it is not clear to what extent the nineteenth-century theories of evolution in biology laid the conceptual ground for twentieth-century thought at large. But no reader of James' *Principles* could fail to come away from the book without the sense that adjustment to change is a major component of psychology. Understand that and you understand a great deal of the prospectus of the science of mind to come. Adjustment to change also provides a tenuous and nebulous link to evolutionary theory, though one which does not take the form of any specific application of the theory to any specific aspect of, or problem in, psychology.

But a crisis was looming in the new science, and unsurprisingly, its roots were in that most basic issue of what it is that one should be studying in psychology. Change, yes. But change of what? Here there was great uncertainty. Wundt had established psychology as the science of experience, of some realm of consciousness deriving from and contributing to sensation, because that is what he thought he could lay his hands on methodologically. It is now claimed that Wundt's stance was wrongly depicted by Boring's influential history. Wundt did not advocate merely a single method, introspection, and what he saw as the scope of psychology was broader (remember his Volkerpsychologie) than that portrayed by his disciple in America, Edward Titchener (who called his brand of psychology "structuralism," not to be confused with the school of thought bearing the same name that rose to prominence in the social sciences in the 1950s and 1960s). Nonetheless, much as can be made of Wundt's broadness of approach, and of his origins in physiology under the tutelage of du Bois-Reymond and Helmholtz, both of whom were convinced physicalists and so rejected outright the dualism of the Cartesians, Wundt's stance on the mind–brain issue as well as the position taken by many subsequent psychologists, was ambiguous. He espoused the psychophysical parallelism of Leibniz who 150 years before had argued for the existence of monads, which make up the known universe in all its forms, each of which is possessed of coordinated but separate physical and conscious mental components. This is not like Descartes' dualism, which was explicit and absolute. There is, wrote Descartes, *res extensa* (body substance) and *res cogitans* (mind substance), and while they might interact, they are different things. This is not the case with psychophysical parallelism which leaves open the issue of just how different mind and body are. It is one of many responses to Descartes' dualism which manages not only to fail to assert that mind and body are one, but recognizes that each is somehow a separate realm, yet not so separate as Descartes maintained. It is a form of fence-sitting which at once claims some form of weak materialism while acknowledging at the same time a difference between mind and body. In essence it is a weak dualism and this is the position that Wundt adopted, as do many psychologists down to the present day. Most will vehemently deny that they are dualists by maintaining that the mind **is** the body, specifically the brain and peripheral nervous system, but claiming at the same time that the mind can be studied without regard to the body. That is either a mightily confident materialism, or a refusal to put the thesis to the test. These days modern technology, like functional imaging of the brain, is perhaps allowing a stronger and more testable materialism in practice to emerge, but a century ago these were methods that no one could dream of.

James himself was equivocal on the mind–body problem. He defined psychology as the science of mental life: "the definition of Psychology may be best given in the words of Professor Ladd, as the *description and explanation of states of consciousness as such*" (italics in the original), he wrote, explaining that "states of consciousness...meant such things as sensations, desires, cognitions, reasonings, decisions, volitions, and the like." As noted in an earlier chapter, he had much to say about consciousness, which he certainly did explicitly link to "an activity of some sort in the cerebral hemispheres." But this was a promissory note written on the expectation that techniques would eventually develop by which details of brain activity could be accessed, and tied to material and certain evidence about consciousness. But the former were then unavailable, and the latter of dubious quality. It did not help that some 15 years later he was to question whether consciousness exists at all.

Baar notes what a strange science psychology is, and was then. Sensations, cognitions, volitions, and the like sit inside each one of us, and are accessible directly, if accessible at all, only to ourselves. We make working assumptions in daily life about the states of mind of others using a broad range of evidence. It mostly works, but it is not science. That broad range of evidence comes from a confusion of social interaction that was not a part of the armory of psychologists in the early 1900s, as well as voiced introspection: "I see blue," or worse, "I know you are disappointed" may or may not be believed in everyday exchanges. The reaction against instrospectionist psychology was that it is not on its own acceptable as evidence of much in science, even if the raw data of all of psychology, including areas as distant and enveloping as memory and vision, is the individual expression of subjective sensations. The problem is that it is just not public and counts for nothing if it is not supported by other, material, publicly verifiable data. It is also of no use when trying to understand psychological processes and mechanisms that are unconscious, and more and more evidence was accumulating for the existence of these. Nor was it a method for studying the minds of infants, of adults with seriously impaired mental states, or of animals. The latter especially began to play a pivotal role in the further development of psychology.

Experimentation, the systematic manipulation of variables under close scrutiny, is not, of course, the only method available to science. Astronomers, after all, do no experiments. But experiments are powerful, and at the start of the twentieth century a broad range of experimental methods began to develop in American psychology, especially in the study of animals. It began with the work on learned behavior in cats by Edward Thorndike at Columbia University. Extending Romanes' observations on the manipulation of latches by cats and dogs to open doors, Thorndike carried out the first systematic experimental study of trial-and-error learning. He later extended his experiments to imitation and passive learning, widely held to be a crucial form of learning, especially in humans. Other experimental methods delved into problem solving, memory and what senses are used in specific forms of learning. One of the principals in this work was Herbert Spencer Jennings, whose doctor father was obviously an enthusiastic philosopher (and evolutionist – he named another son Darwin, Boakes tells us). Another major animal experimentalist was John B. Watson (1878–1958), whose effects on the direction psychology was to take for almost 50 years was momentous – a direction quite away from evolutionary biology.

Watson arrived at the University of Chicago, a powerful center of the new science of psychology, in 1901 to do graduate research. His earliest studies were explicitly physiologically oriented and measured learning in the white rat, an animal newly arrived in American laboratories. His methods were an extension of those of Thorndike and he proved a dedicated and careful researcher. Awarded his doctorate in 1903 he went on to study a range of problems, including visual perception in a variety of animals, primates amongst them. He met and impressed James Mark Baldwin, a rising star in American psychology, and Robert Yerkes, another of the coming young scientists then at Harvard. It is of particular interest, in the light of what was to come, that Watson also carried out some pioneering naturalistic studies on the wild of the behavior of terns, species of sea birds. He wanted to know how birds that nest communally are able to locate their own nests, recognize their partners, and how the behavior of the adults changes when their eggs hatch. He was a meticulous observer and also began to carry out small-scale experiments under these free-living conditions. In this Watson was anticipating by 50 and more years classic studies on gull behavior by ethologists.

Watson's reputation grew. In 1908 Baldwin offered him a Professorship at John Hopkins University and Watson moved from Chicago to Baltimore. The following year Baldwin had to resign his position because of a scandal (see next chapter) and Watson found himself propelled into being the substitute for the disgraced Baldwin both as Chair of the department of psychology at John Hopkins and as an editor of the *Psychological Review*, much the most important professional journal for the new science. With Knight Dunlap and Jennings already at John Hopkins, and with the later arrivals of Adolf Meyer and Karl Lashley, both of whom became very important to the development of understanding of psychopathology and brain-behavior relationships respectively, Watson was suddenly a man of consequence.

In 1913 Watson was invited to lecture at Columbia University. It was an invitation that was to change psychology. Watson had long been bothered by people asking him what the relevance of his animal work was to the understanding of humans. After all, animals cannot supply introspective reports of their experiences, and intellectually fastidious observers had become fatigued by outrageous claims for consciousness in nonhumans, which even the likes of Yerkes was speculating upon with regard to plants! The situation was becoming indefensible and embarrassing for anyone with a sense of being a serious scientist. Watson, despite his naturalistic studies, had no time for evolution (not because of religious scruples, he simply thought it without interest or relevance to psychology) and so was unprepared to answer his questioners with the kind of principle of specific application that Romanes or Morgan would have given, vague as it was, that all species derive from a common lineage. He could either respond by saying the behaviors of rats, monkeys, or terns are interesting in their own right and that he is simply doing biology. Or he could provide a reason for working on animals that had application to humans. He chose the latter and devoted his Columbia lectures to it.

Watson's conceptual move comprised two parts. The first was to reject absolutely all reports, interpretations, or speculation on inner mental states as the basis for psychology. Let's have done, he said, with arguments about consciousness, whether it exists, and if it does, just what it is. Only that which is publicly observable and manifestly material, **behavior**, is the proper data of a scientific psychology. Behavior can be directly seen and measured in innumerable ways. In making this move, Watson shifted psychology towards the stance of a philosophical school known as logical positivism, with its verifiability criterion of meaning, which demands that every genuine contingent assertion about the world must be tied, verified, by as direct experience and observation as possible. The second part of Watson's move followed from the first. If behavior is the proper subject matter of psychology, why then the study of animals becomes directly transferable to the understanding of humans.

Watson gave his talk and later in 1913 published the first of them in *Psychological Review*, which as editor would have presented little difficulty. Entitled "Psychology as the behaviorist views it" the opening paragraph stated:

> Psychology as the behaviorist views it is a purely objective experimental branch of natural science. Its theoretical goal is the prediction and control of behavior. Introspection forms no essential part of its methods, nor is the scientific value of its data dependent upon the readiness with which they lend themselves to interpretation in terms of consciousness. The behaviorist, in his efforts to get a unitary scheme of animal response, recognizes no dividing line between man and brute. The behavior of man, with all its refinement and complexity, forms only part of the behaviorist's total scheme of investigation. (Watson, 1913, p. 158)

Later, a decade after he had left academic life and was working with great success in advertising, he famously wrote:

> Give me a dozen healthy infants, well-formed and my own specified world to bring them up in and I'll guarantee to take any one at random and train him to become any type of specialist I might select – doctor, lawyer, artist, merchant-chief and, yes, even beggar-man and thief, regardless of his talents, penchants, tendencies, abilities, vocations, and race of his ancestors. (Watson, 1924, p. 104)

Several points about Watson's behaviorism must be made. The first is that the primary claim is on "prediction and control of behavior," and not a causal explanation of that behavior (though behaviorists argued that control implies an understanding of causation – it may, but if it does it is incomplete causal understanding). It takes little thought to realize that even introspective reports are a form of behavior, and in that sense, psychology's methods from the outset had been concerned with measurable behavior. But what Watson did was abandon the attempt to explain that behavior by something other than what could be directly observed. This form of peripheralism was forced by his extraordinary crucial claim that "there are no centrally initiated processes." Emotions were the result of events occurring in organs like genitalia, and thought was subvocal speech – a kind of twitching of the vocal cords. He actually wrote that a man "who lost his laryngeal apparatus without any serious injury to the other bodily mechanisms" would be deprived of the capacity for thought. This should have been easy enough to test; that it was not suggests that psychologists took some aspects of Watson's behaviorism with a pinch of salt, even if they did tend to buy in to the whole package.

Another feature of behaviorism, which was to be even more strongly adhered to by most of his followers than was his prescription for dispensing with explanation, was an emphasis on empiricist associationism of the Locke–Hume kind. His famous "give me a dozen healthy infants" claim, even though he admitted to having no evidence to support it, was as plain a statement of a *tabula rasa* position as one can get; and in 1913, and onwards for the next 30 or 40 years, the only forms of learning behaviorists seriously considered by which the slate is written on was associationism of one kind or another. This places Pavlov's work in a proper perspective. When it finally became widely known in the United States in the 1920s, conditioning stood alongside trial-and-error learning, of the kind Thorndike had experimented on, as the two forms of association learning that dominated behaviorist thought. Stimuli, responses, and reinforcement (reward and punishment), and elaborations upon these, became the staple conceptual diet for large tracts of psychology.

Watson was involved in personal scandal and like Baldwin before him, he left American academic life but, unlike Baldwin, remained in the USA and continued to write popular books. Watson had somehow hit the right note at the right time. Support for his approach was to come from two directions. The first was the social environment of the United States. This was a society that believed in getting things done and hang the explanation, especially if that explanation seems to live so close to philosophy.

In an intensely practical environment, behaviorism promised to deliver understanding on practical issues like how better to educate children, raise them as effective citizens, and to help directly those afflicted by psychopathology. It also broke upon the world during the World War One when anti-German feeling was intense and patriotism peaking. Here was a home-grown science of behavior which owed nothing to the mystical notions of mind so favored by Europeans.

The second was that it chimed well with the subsequent rise of operationalism and logical positivism in philosophy of science. Percy Bridgman had advocated that theoretical concepts be identified with the operations used to measure them. This was exactly what the behaviorists who came after Watson did, especially B.F. Skinner, and it was averred to attract the support of logical positivists and philosophical behaviorists like Carnap, Wittgenstein and, later, Ryle. In science, especially a fledgling science, it is a good thing to be able to claim to have illustrious names like these to back your position.

Further support for behaviorism came from the abysmal failure of instinct theory in the early part of the twentieth century. Instinct theory (and theory is really too grand a word for what this was) in the period leading up to 1920 has its origins in the failure of Darwin and others in sorting out the relationship between instincts and intelligence. As shown in chapter 3, one way of dealing with instincts was to consider them, as Darwin did, as behavioral equivalents of corporeal structures. They were automatic, unlearned behaviors that evolved from a history of selection pressures in the same way as any other adaptive trait did. If there was continuity between species, then it followed that the age-old distinction, between instincts as being confined to animals and only humans are intelligent and rational, be abandoned. But in failing to understand the relationship between learning and instinct, the distinction was abandoned in an odd way. After Darwin, people began to search for intelligence in animals, and soon found it; they also began to look for instincts in humans – and claims about these began to abound. At first they were presented within some semblance of a disciplined framework, even if empirical support was lacking. Part of the ghost of Darwin in James' *Principles* was his advocacy of instincts as "impulses" to action of a "reflex type." Compared to what was to come over the next few decades, his advocacy of instincts was restrained, and he considered many to be modifiable by learning. Somewhat less guarded was William McDougal, an English academic, who published a book in 1908 which was built on the notion that humans are possessed of seven instincts: these were flight and fear, repulsion and disgust, curiosity and wonder, pugnacity and anger, self-abasement and subjection, self-assertion and elation, and parental and tender emotions. It is odd that motivational states regarding food, water, and other basic requirements of life were omitted. Apart from a form of literary analysis of what humans get up to, no evidence was presented to support his position. Worse was to come. Boakes records that "in the first twenty years of the [twentieth] century, four hundred authors of books or articles had proposed nearly six thousand classes of instinct encompassing over fourteen thousand individual cases." The procedure was simple enough. If a group of people were thought to exhibit a common behavior or objective, and if that group were arbitrarily judged to be above a certain number, then that was taken to be evidence of an instinct. One example that Boakes gives is the instinct to free the Christian subjects of the Sultan, an "instinct" with some nasty overtones. Early genetic concepts were used to supply ill-judged justification for the notion of instinct and the idea spread to take in national and ethnic differences. Race theory abounded and fed off, and strengthened, racial prejudices. Few were invoking culture as an alternative explanation of what was being claimed.

The behaviorists would have none of what was outrageously bad science, if it was science at all. The bases of instincts were not publicly observable. The entire notion of instinct ran counter to the empiricism of behaviorism which, as an idea whose time had come, simply steam-rolled one of the sillier and more shameful episodes in psychology's history. The inevitable collapse of instinct theory added to the impetus of behaviorism. Boring put it this way: "Some conservatives were Wundtian, some radicals were functionalists, more psychologists were agnostics. Then Watson touched a match to the mass, there was an explosion, and only behaviorism was left" (in Baars, 1986, p.41). It would be wrong to say that from 1920 to the late 1950s behaviorism ruled absolutely. It did not. Personality theory, psychometrics, social psychology, and clinical study thrived. But it is certainly the case that experimental psychology in the United States came to be dominated by behaviorism and its assumptions. Watson quickly became a spent force, but after his departure other powerful figures like Clark L. Hull, Edward Tolman, and Skinner took his place. The central tenets of psychology, its *sanctum sanctorum*, was that psychology as science is based on what happens in muscles and other peripheral organs, and on how a few basic reflexes are elaborated by experience, either by conditioning or a history of reinforcement contingencies, to result in observable behavior.

Behaviorism represented the unconstrained triumph of empiricism. Nurture and blank slates ruled, evolution was gone, and so too was the rationalism of Plato and Descartes.

The Rise of Cultural Anthropology

In 1912 Franz Boas (1858–1942) published a report which showed that the cranial index could be significantly altered by environmental conditions. The cranial index is the ratio between head breadth and head length, and is easily and quickly measured with spreading calipers, given a modicum of cooperation from individual subjects, by people with no particular expertise. In the nineteenth century the ratio had been established as a reliable measure, and identifier, of human "race" and was considered to be caused wholly by innate factors. In twentieth-century parlance, whether one is dolichocephelic (long-headed), brachycephalic (broad-headed) or something in between was genetically determined and racially fixed. Thus Boas' results were something of a sensation. He had had measured the heads of some 13,000 European immigrants and their children from seven ethnic groups (ranging from Scottish to Italian, with the largest being Jews from Eastern Europe, whom Boas referred to as Hebrews), the principal comparisons being both between groups, and importantly, within groups in which children born in Europe were compared to children of the same parents born in the United States. Boas claimed to show that all children born in the United States began to "approach a uniform type," with the long-headed becoming more broad-headed and vice versa. Boas was elated because he was the General of a small army fighting against the cause of absolute genetic determination of fixed racial differences which was then being advanced by a much larger force of eugenicists and racist ideologues. According to the latter, whose cry was "nature not nurture," Boas should never have been able to record changes in the cephalic index of different groups. For Boas this was a triumphant vindication of his contrary view that "the social stimulus is infinitely more potent than the biological mechanism."

It is clear from the language that more was at stake here than science. In 2002 and 2003 publications appeared from two separate groups of investigators both of whom had independently reanalyzed Boas' original data, having the advantage of much improved statistical methods of analysis. One group publishing in the *Proceedings of the National Academy of Sciences* concluded that their results "point to very small and insignificant differences between European-and American-born offspring, and no effect of exposure to the American environment on the cranial index in children." The other study, published in the *American Anthropologist*, begged to differ, because "in general, we conclude that Boas got it right." That neither group considers the findings of the other incorrect, that the index has high heritability **and** that there were differences, albeit very small, between American- and European-born children, but that each draws different conclusions as to what the data set tells us scientifically, speaks loudly to how, 90 years on, it remains the case that interpretations of complex findings are subject to ideological filters – that people will find support for the position that they favor, and that the science may be distorted or misunderstood. As Degler concludes, though right at the beginning of his comprehensive survey of twentieth-century American social thought: "What the available evidence does seem to show is that ideology or a philosophical belief that the world could be a freer and more just place played a large part in the shift from biology to culture" in the period from around 1910 to 1930. By then, despite legalized sterilization in both the United States, Canada, and four European countries, most notoriously in Germany in 1933 (though the legislation had begun before the rise of the National Socialists to power), eugenics and racial theories of human history were discredited doctrines.

It began with Darwin's 1871 book. It will be remembered from chapter 3 that in that book Darwin's principal aim was to show that humans are descended from apes, and that we share a great many psychological and social features with other hominids.

That was his main message. Indeed, given that a form of human race evolution had already emerged, for example in the work of the anthropologist Tylor, based on the essential notion that races are inherently different, be that difference a result of either natural selection *à la* Darwin or different because of deviations resulting from Lamarckian–Spencerian evolutionary history, and that the differences verge on incipient species differences, Darwin specifically sets out to refute this. Yet Darwin was a man of his age and his age was one of casual and rampant racism. He fully subscribed to the notion that Europeans were a superior people than those of Africa, the native peoples of the Americas, or the Orient, and his language would today be ruled wholly politically incorrect. Whilst considering slavery an evil on the one hand, on the other he was not averse to referring to "savages who delight(s) to torture his enemies, offer(s) up blood sacrifices." But one must see past this rhetoric of European superiority. Darwin drew attention "to the numerous points of mental similarity between the most distinct races of man." And he concluded that:

> important as the struggle for existence has been and even still is, yet as far as the highest parts of man's nature is concerned *there are other agencies more important*. For the moral qualities are advanced, either directly or indirectly, much more through the effects of habit, the reasoning powers, instruction, religion, etc., than through natural selection; though to this latter agency may be safely attributed the social instincts, which afforded the basis for the development of the moral sense. (Darwin, 1871, p. 919; italics added)

Darwin's insight was profound, given that at that time there was simply no widespread conception of culture as a system of shared knowledge. He understood that all humans are biologically equal, and all possess evolved "social instincts."

So Darwin's position was clear. Racial difference was not a product of evolutionary forces, all humans are fundamentally the same, and what differences there are between social groups result from habit, instruction, and reasoning. Yet he wrote with an undisguised contempt for non-European societies and thus laid open the way for racial evolutionary theorists, be they the Galtons of that Victorian world or the Ernst Haeckels. The latter makes an interesting contrast with Boas. Haeckel was 24 years older than Boas and was another of Darwin's German champions but he was an explicit racist and anti-Semite who believed that racial differences were irremediably fixed by inheritance, that "inferior" races were intermediate between apes and Aryans, and that it was natural selection that had driven these differences.

Boas, however, had grown up in a liberal humanitarian household steeped in the ideals of the 1848 revolution. He had taken in with his mother's milk the notion that all people are the same and all should be treated as equals. He graduated in physics from the University of Berlin having also read a great deal of philosophy. He had been much influenced, like so many liberal Europeans, by Kant, who taught that humans were unique in being able to construct their own worlds, and by Wilhelm Dilthey, who drew a sharp distinction between the natural and the human sciences, the latter being accounted for by history and understood within an interpretative framework, not one of scientific measurement. But much the greatest influences on his thinking was Rudolf Virchow, one of the leaders of German anthropology who simply did not believe that humans had evolved from other animals, and Theodore Waitz, who was an outright Lamarckian. Always distrustful of Darwin's theory and of the science of genetics when it came, Boas was much more sympathetic to Lamarck, as were most liberal-minded social scientists of the time. This was for the simple reason that whereas the social Darwinists (not Darwin, remember, who was not a social Darwinist) considered race differences to be fixed by inheritance, the Spencerian vision of evolving societies progressing from the primitive to the civilized by way of the Lamarckian inheritance of acquired characters meant that race differences could be overcome by appropriate manipulation of the environment. Thus despite the justification by the social Darwinist of exploitation of the poor and backward by the rich and powerful in terms of Spencer's "survival of the fittest" slogan, Spencer also gave comfort to social liberals. There seemed to be no end to the confusion sown by Spencer.

In the 1880s Boas traveled to the arctic and was fascinated by the habits and traditions of the Eskimo people amongst whom he lived. That experience settled his future direction, and in 1899 was appointed a professor of anthropology at Columbia University, after publishing some of the most seminal papers in the short history of his discipline. One of the most important, "On

Alternating Sounds," concerned the difficulties that nonnative speakers of a language had when encountering a foreign language. This resulted in a characteristic "sound blindness," an inability to discriminate the variety of sounds associated with a new language and a perception of its having alternating sound patterns. Boas argued that, contrary to the prevailing view that this was a characteristic of primitive languages being detected by European observers, it was in fact a universal condition of everyone's perception of an unfamiliar language, including that of so-called "primitives" on first hearing "advanced" languages like English and German. In a letter to *Science* in 1887 he wrote that "civilization is not something absolute...it is relative...our ideas and conceptions are true only so far as our civilization goes." Freeman notes that in 1907 Boas, despite his proselytizing for the power of culture as a system of social inheritance, asserted in a lecture that no separation was possible between anthropological, biological, and psychological conceptions and methods, and that measured scientific study was what was needed to put each in its place. He pleaded for the prohibition of the political and the ideological from the science of man, but he was to be denied that relief.

From both sides of the Atlantic the clamor from race theorists and eugenicists was reaching a crescendo. In England respectability for eugenics came with university posts and courses devoted to the subject. In 1910 the geneticist Charles Davenport, secretary of the Committee on Eugenics of the American Breeders Association, proclaimed that only eugenics could "redeem mankind from vice, imbecility and suffering," and that "the betterment of the human race" (a word of unsure meaning) depended on "better matings." Both Degler and Freeman note that the case for eugenics was made with an extraordinary zeal and fervor verging on a religious crusade. By 1915 Davenport was arguing for specific genetic causes of a host of behaviors frowned on by polite society, and in 1916 Madison Grant's *The Passing of the Great Race*, a title potently sinister, was published and praised. With the discovery of chromosomes at around this time adding impetus to the sense that genetics was all-powerful and all-knowing as a science, dozens of American universities began to offer courses on eugenics: these included Harvard, The Massachusetts Institute of Technology, and Chicago. In 1907 legal sterilization of the genetically unfit, i.e. of the criminal and the insane, was introduced in Indiana. By 1915 it had been introduced in a further 12 states and by 1930, 30 states of the Union had enacted such laws. As noted earlier, it had by then also become legal in Canada and some European countries. In a landmark judgment of the United States Supreme Court in 1927 on involuntary sterilization in Virginia, Justice Oliver Wendell Holmes declared that "It is better for all the world if instead of waiting to execute degenerate offspring for crime, or let them starve for their imbecility, society can prevent those who are manifestly unfit from continuing their kind." It was against this background that Boas moved from a reasoned middle position to an extreme form of culturalism.

Boas' *The Mind of Primitive Man* of 1911 argued that "the psychological basis of cultural traits is identical in all races," and that culture is the ruling force in determining human behavior. Forty years earlier Wallace himself had mused on the unlikelihood that natural selection had played much part in the later stages of human evolution, and had expressed the view that "savage" or "primitive" peoples had mental capacities no different from those who are civilized. Thomas Huxley in his Romanes lecture of 1893 had speculated that the evolution of society was a process "essentially different from that which brought about the evolution of species"; and in 1899 E.R. Lankester, the then Director of the British Museum of Natural History, had written about humankind's educability giving rise to a huge mass of "accumulated experience, knowledge, tradition, custom and law" that envelopes any and all social groups. As Freeman notes, therefore, at the start of the twentieth century, Boas was not alone in contemplating two evolutionary systems, one biological and one social, the extent of whose interaction needed close study. But Boas' position a dozen years on was being forced by the unremitting weight of propaganda by the race theorists and eugenicists. Hence his interpretation of his cranial index study and his move towards a complete break with biology.

Boas' position was straight forward and simple. There just was no evidence, he argued, for the strong hereditarian position that placed the biological forces of genetics and selection as supreme, and social forces as minimal in determining human nature and action. Culture is extragenetic, works identically in all social groups, results in differences in different social groups because of differences in history, and as a force in humans is far, far greater than that of biology. Boas was right in pointing to the lack of evidence for the supremacy of biology in determining what people are and do. What he failed to see was that there was equally no evidence to support his claim for the overwhelming importance of the social. It is easy with hindsight to understand the futility of the claims and counter-claims of each side. Just look at the absurdly opposite interpretations of modern reanalyzes of his cephalic index data. But it is also easy to understand the intolerable pressures from a rampant and unreconstructed primitive biologism that so goaded him.

Boas's students, Kroeber and Lowie, completed the swing of anthropological opinion to the dominating view that anthropology as a science was to be pursued by the study of culture and the minimalizing of biological factors. The dominance was not complete; in the social sciences it never is. But the collapse of the eugenics movement added to the impetus of the conceptual move. There were several reasons why eugenics, at one time believed in by an astonishing array of leading intellectuals, statesmen, and even socialists, collapsed. One was the unremitting hostility within psychology to the then discredited notion of instincts, with its underlying hereditarian assumptions. Watson's colleague Dunlap was to write an influential paper asking "Are there any instincts?" Another was that the mental test movement in America, which had been a powerful tool for the eugenicists was no less discredited by 1930. More importantly, as more became known about genetics, so the powerful aims of the movement receded from the realms of the possible. Genes, it was found, are not invariable in expression. Moreover, with few exceptions, "feeble-mindedness" is not caused by single genes, and nor, without exceptions, is criminality. And even if they were, because recessive genes are expressed in only a minority of those possessing them, it was calculated that thousands of years of selective breeding would be needed to eradicate them completely. These were powerful reasons for causing faith in the movement to be lost. But finally, and most importantly, abhorrence took root and spread at the idea that human beings, even if mentally damaged or impaired in some way, should be forcibly prevented from the joy of having children. The vile events in Germany and the consequences of the Nazi occupation of much of Europe which linked eugenics with genocide could not, of course, be foreseen by the cultural determinists, but they were a vindication of the view that eugenics was an evil doctrine.

Almost single-handedly Boas had created a science of culture which owed little to biology and whose central tenets were social history and social inheritance. If the world had been kinder, it might have been a more balanced science than it was to be for the next 40 to 50 years. In the event, anthropology was more "de-biologized" by the culturalists than was psychology by the behaviorists. The combined effects of the behaviorists and the cultural determinists was to reduce to near invisibility the presence of biology in general, and evolutionary theory specifically, in the social sciences. With the exception to be outlined in the next chapter, evolutionary theory ceases to have any application in psychology until the 1960s.

CHAPTER FIVE

An Exceptional Case

James Mark Baldwin (1861–1934) is a very important and unique figure in the history of psychology. That he has faded into insignificance is not the least interesting aspect of the man and tells us something of the importance of seeing science within a social context, because, for a time, Baldwin was that rare thing before the 1980s – he was a "real" evolutionary psychologist for whom the theory of evolution marked one of the essential conceptual lines onto which an adequate theory of psychology had to be mapped. The vague functionalism of William James finds no expression in Baldwin's psychology. For Baldwin, evolution was an absolute conceptual anchor. Baldwin was singular in other ways. For one thing, he is the only psychologist in the history of the discipline to have had a major impact on the theory of evolution itself, even if on a debatable issue, and that is no mean feat. For another, Baldwin discovered cognitive developmental stages in humans which differ qualitatively from one another. In this he was the father of modern developmental psychology. Third, it might be argued that he anticipated the concept of Theory of Mind and its importance to the process of enculturation and so may also be considered the father of social psychology. Finally, he was a major contributor to evolutionary epistemology. For all these reasons, Baldwin is perhaps the most significant person in the history of the relationship between evolutionary theory and psychology. Certainly no one did more to disambiguate the relationship between evolution, behavior, and learning than Baldwin, and hence to repair the damage done by Spencer.

Born into small-town America in South Carolina at the start of the Civil War, Baldwin was raised as a strict Presbyterian and went to college with a view to becoming a clergyman. A clever young man, he found his way to Princeton where he came under the influence of the Scottish realist intuitionist philosopher James McCosh. Always much inclined towards philosophy, in the final year of his undergraduate degree he wrote a thesis on *a priori* theories of conscience, a suitable mix of science and moral philosophy, on the basis of which he won a Fellowship which allowed him to travel in Europe for a year. He spent over half of that time in Wundt's psychology laboratory and became an enthusiast of the new science, even if not of the methods of introspection. He also spent time in Berlin where he came into contact with Spinoza's ideas, which reinforced his view that a science of mind had to be founded, and could be so founded, on a solid philosophical, as well as an empirical, base. It was to this task that he first turned his attention when he returned to the United States.

Baldwin's academic progress was swift. In 1889 he was appointed to a chair of psychology at the University of Toronto, where he established an experimental laboratory. He returned to Princeton in 1893, and finally moved to John Hopkins in 1903 to which, as described in the previous chapter, he enticed Watson. Along the way he cofounded the *Psychological Review*, which rapidly became, and continues to be, the most prestigious journal of theoretical psychology in the world. He also established several other journals, edited a huge *Dictionary of Philosophy and Psychology*, and wrote a number of important books and seminal journal papers.

Whilst responsible for establishing or directing three laboratories, and carrying out several different lines of experimentation, including one on handedness, Baldwin's contribution was not, with the exception of the observations he made within his own family, empirical. He was, by contrast, passionate about the importance of theory, and it is one of psychology's great ironies that Baldwin played so significant a role in the elevation of the arch antitheorist, John Watson. Because of the range of his theoretical contributions it is useful, if somewhat artificial, to consider each in relative separation from the others.

The Fundamental Problem

Baldwin's earliest efforts were directed to building a philosophically defensible psychology centered on epistemology. Baldwin was concerned (remember this was still the nineteenth century) with establishing a monism of mind and body, and crucially of mind and the material world, the world outside of the organism. To this end he built upon Spinoza's substantive monism, which was expressed by the seventeenth-century Dutch philosopher in a form of pantheism which identified God with nature, and nineteenth-century French spiritualist philosophy which dealt with various ways of bending philosophical analyses such as those of Spinoza or Kant in conformity with the findings of empirical science. What Baldwin was after was a monism stripped of a religious metaphysics by which he could establish what Robert Wozniak calls a "coordinative epistemology" between what is in the mind and what is in the material world, and he believed that he had done so. In 1887 he wrote: "To say that the soul is natural . . . is to say that nature is intelligent and that the laws of thought are the laws of things." This is a thoroughly materialistic position, and one can only assume that its publication in the *Presbyterian Review* reflected some need on Baldwin's part to reconcile his science with his upbringing, and perhaps to maintain a hold on his early spiritualist leanings. More to the point, what he was doing in these early years was laying the foundation for the view that we, and in an extended sense all intelligent organisms, really can have valid knowledge in our minds of what is out there in the world. What we know, he was claiming, has validity by virtue of our expectations and habits working in and on the world. But this was not just a form of pragmatism. Baldwin was not afraid to use the word truth, but nor was he simple-minded about it. He recognized that the richness of the world meant that our knowledge of it, truth, is not constant but changing, developing, and evolving. Our ability to know, and that ability constantly to gain knowledge, he considered itself to be a product of evolution, and hence his position was strongly nativist or rationalist. However, it was also, despite its understanding that knowledge is constantly shifting, a kind of static view in the sense that prior to 1888 he was looking for a preestablished coordination between reason and experience, a coordination established by evolution; one that, by way of fixed evolved cognitive structures, is constant in operation across our lives, though differing, of course, in content. Then in 1888, a year before his move to Toronto, Baldwin's first child, a daughter, was born. In 1891 a second daughter was born. Closely observing his children forced a radical change in his thinking.

Baldwin was not the first developmental psychologist. Wilhelm Preyer, a German psychologist, had published *The Mind of the Child* in 1882, which after its translation into English was widely read in the United States. Preyer's work was based on Haekel's biogenetic principle of recapitulation, summed up by the phrase "ontogeny recapitulates phylogeny": in short, the notion that the development of the individual repeats the evolution of its species. Recapitulation theories received much attention in the first half-century after the publication of Darwin's *Origin* and are now largely dismissed as inaccurate and irrelevant, if not plain wrong when they are constructed, as most were, on Lamarckian evolutionary principles. Preyer's book was thus an exercise in seeing the development of the child's mind in terms of the evolution of the psychological characteristics of *Homo sapiens*. A similar stance was taken by G. Stanley Hall, the founding professor of psychology at John Hopkins University and hence a seminal figure in the history of psychology. Hall's "genetic psychology" (this was nearly 20 years before the discovery of Mendel's work, so genetic referred to origins not to genes), like that of Preyer, was based on Lamarckian principles. This certainly was an instance of specific application of evolutionary theory to psychology, but it was the wrong evolutionary theory. Baldwin, by contrast, was an avowed Darwinian.

In order to appreciate Baldwin's originality, it is necessary to understand the general context within which children in general, and their minds specifically, were viewed at that time. That children were generally seen as miniature adults well into the nineteenth century is widely understood and documented. The empiricists, and their associationist brethren in psychology, promulgated the notion that the only difference between the mind of a child and that of an adult lay in the number and richness of associations formed. The strong rationalist or nativist position, which was that of Baldwin before the birth of his children, with its emphasis upon innate *a prioris* of causality, space, time, number, and capacity for learning and reasoning, similarly minimized any differences between adult and child. So what Baldwin observed in his children was a revelation for him, and the beginnings of a revolution in psychology. Whilst in their bodies and limbs infants and young children appear to be miniature adults, in their minds they are most certainly not. The reason and understanding, the coordination of the mind with the external world, of a 6-or 16-month-old infant are different, Baldwin realized, from each other, and each is different from that of an adult. What in the twenty-first century may seem obvious and banal was not so in 1890. It was a completely novel discovery.

Baldwin had to rethink his position, but he never wavered in his monism or his commitment to evolutionary theory. In *Mental Development in the Child and Race* of 1895 he provided the first definitive statement of genetic (again in the sense of origins) psychology. In place of the mind as a fixed something, whatever that something is, we have to have "the conception of a growing, developing activity." Mind is the product not just of an evolved phylogenetic history but of an ontogenetic history as well. The world may be constant but thought changes. Reason is a developing capacity of mind. This may sound like a repackaged Spencer but it was not. Baldwin was no Lamarckian, and he clearly demarcated nature (evolution) from nurture (individual development and experience), whilst fully understanding how closely they hinged upon one another. In this he was decades beyond his time. Furthermore, observing his children, Baldwin described specific cognitive developmental stages, each building upon the last, each different from previous stages, and each based upon a repetitive, constructive process.

Baldwin developed the notion of a circular action or process as a necessary and constructive function. By this is meant that in order to get, epistemologically, from where we are now to some future state of knowledge and understanding, we use a repetitive process that imperfectly circles (elliptically, would be the appropriate imagery) from where we are, incorporating or assimilating new variations, to enable us to reach where we are going, which is a new set of structures. These new knowledge structures are connected, by accommodation, to what the old structures were, and central to the entire process is a general conception of imitation: "... the stimulus starts a motor process which tends to reproduce the stimulus and, through it, the motor process again," but since imitative acts are never exact repetitions of one another, the process is dynamic and keeps changing the knowledge structures.

In positing repetitive circular acts, in emphasizing the central role of action on the world, and in using the notions of assimilation and accommodation (sometimes the very words themselves), Baldwin anticipated Jean Piaget by 30 years and more.

In developing these ideas of repetition and variation, the latter being internally selected "so as to adapt the organism better" and hence drive an ontogeny of knowledge, Baldwin for the first time uses the phrase **organic selection** to describe an ever more adequate comprehension of the world, a more detailed and deep coordination of knowledge with reality. The capacity of this progressive individual development to result in an increasingly valid or true coordination of reason and reality has itself been selected for in the history of our species. This is an emphatically Darwinian monism which evokes selection as a crucial internal (within-organism) as well as external (between-organism) process. Baldwin never fell into the Lamarckism which Piaget, using a remarkably similar conceptual toolbox, was later to do.

In a *Science* paper of 1891, Baldwin revealed an interest in relating cognitive development in infancy with hypnosis and "suggestion," which he broadly defined as the tendency for a stimulus to be followed by a motor response, as a means of getting at the problem of consciousness in very young children and its role in cognitive ontogeny. He used this rather odd connection to suggest a specific sequence of cognitive developmental stages to account for what he was seeing in his children. The first, unconscious, stage is a physiological integration between stimuli and motor habits; the second is a conscious sensori-motor stage; and the third an ideo-motor stage, subdivided into simple (reflexive) and persistent imitation, the last of which, persistent imitative action, results from the infant voluntarily varying and guiding its motor acts in order to match the activity of some model – the child wants consciously to achieve an observed action.

Baldwin was dogged by claims that at least two of his main ideas, of which the centrality of imitation to cognitive development was one (the Baldwin effect, was the other), were really the inventions of others which Baldwin simply appropriated. The truth of this is difficult to judge, not least because, as a proud and rather prickly character, he seemed personally to antagonize his colleagues more than most. Also science is replete with instances of the parallel evolution of concepts, in part because people genuinely cannot untangle in their own minds and memories how their own ideas relate to those of others. This merely repeats the theme of earlier chapters. The history of ideas has no beginning. More to the point, though, these assertions are irrelevant because what matters in science is how well novel concepts are stitched into the fabric of scientific theory, and hence what impact they have, rather than who thought of what first. In this respect Baldwin's genius is further evidenced by his placing his theory of individual cognitive development within a social context, and hence developing a social and cultural psychology out of a developmental framework which again anticipates all others, including the Russian Lev Vygotsky, by 30 years.

In *Mental Development in the Child and the Race*, as well as in numerous other publications, Baldwin developed his realization that it is other people, not the physical world, which is the focus of the child's knowledge gain. It is the behavior of others that is the principal source of imitation, and later it is the ideas and knowledge of others that are acquired. Moreover, it is not just naked facts that are learned. These social interactions result not just in a transmission of knowledge, but also in the formation of the sense of self and others. "My sense of self grows by imitation of you, and my sense of yourself grows in terms of my sense of myself. Both ego and alter are thus essentially social; each is a socius, and *each is an imitative creation*" (italics added). "Imitative creation" captures wonderfully well Baldwin's conceptual marriage of how novel each person's knowledge is, yet how utterly dependent it is on the knowledge of others.

This social transmission of knowledge, which was to become so central to Baldwin's evolutionary epistemology, he thought occurred in three stages of development of consciousness. The first, projective consciousness, results in the child differentiating between people and all other objects. This is followed by subjective consciousness as the child becomes aware of its own subjective states of knowledge and feeling. The final stage is ejective consciousness, whereby the growing child comes to understand that others have subjective mental states too, and that such understanding is the basis for entering into a community of shared knowledge and feeling, that is, for entering into culture. This is no longer merely imitation; this is the social construction of knowledge. Once again Baldwin anticipates, in this case by something like 80 years, the realization in the 1980s of the importance of the attribution of intentional mental states to others, what was to become known as Theory of Mind (ToM), and the developmental sequence by which this is now known to occur.

Furthermore, in positing the crucial role in human life of shared knowledge and beliefs, Boas' culture, Baldwin developed the idea of the "environment of thought" in which ideas are subjected to variation, are selected, and then are transmitted and hence conserved. This form of his evolutionary epistemology is pure memetics (see chapter 7), though memeticists of the 1990s who think they invented the subject know little of Baldwin. Indeed in understanding that "thought variations" do not all have the same status but differ in terms of where they exist within the complex organization of the thought world, and the role that they play, Baldwin was writing a form of memetics much superior to that which is on offer now.

A New Factor in Evolution

In the preface to *Darwin and the Humanities*, perhaps his most readable and broadly based book published in 1909, Baldwin asked "who would not consider it an honour to be allowed to 'claim' that he had done something to carry Darwin's great and illuminating conception into those fields of more general philo-sophical interest, in which in the end its value for human thought must be estimated?" One such achievement, which was intended to transcend specific application to humans but which certainly has consequences for human evolution, was what he termed "organic selection," "a new factor in evolution" as he entitled the first of his journal papers describing it.

Organic selection, as stated earlier, was a term first used in a general way to refer to individual adaptation by learning that conformed to Darwinian processes. It was also used to refer to the way in which ontogenetic adaptations, including those resulting from learning, contributed to individual survival and hence, in this rather nebulous fashion, contributes to evolution. But the new factor in evolution expanded on this usage by asserting a more specific between-individual role, which directly influences the course of evolution at a population and species level – in effect, an additional force by which evolution occurs to those proposed by Darwin. What Baldwin suggested was that environmentally elicited individual phenotypic adaptations might come under genotypic control and hence transmitted via inheritance to offspring. But this was emphatically **not** a form of

Lamarckism. Lamarck, remember, had postulated the inheritance of acquired characters whereby changes in an individual wrought by learning or in some other way results directly in changes in that individual's hereditary material, what Weismann called the germ plasm and what after the discovery of Mendel's work became known as genes, and hence which would be transmitted to that individual's offspring. What Baldwin was postulating was a **coincident** correspondence between chance hereditary changes and their phenotypic effects with the effects of individual ontogenetic adaptations, with the former then replacing the latter. So what makes Baldwin's new factor wholly un-Lamarckian is that the changes in the genotype are chance-based, what would soon become known as undirected mutations of genes.

Consider the simple example of a group of organisms suddenly subjected to environmental conditions which their phenotypic plasticity allows them to adapt to through ontogenetic means, perhaps by learning. It might, for instance, be a learned dietary preference. These ontogenetic adaptations are not directly inherited and evolved and hence innate; the capacity for forming them, of course, is evolved and inherited. Such indirect adaptations ensure survival over enough generations for chance-based genetic changes to occur which fit with, supplement, or perhaps produce identical phenotypic effects. Eventually such genetic modification would produce the same, or very similar adaptations, and the indirect, ontogenetic adaptations become redundant. The learned dietary preference becomes innate. The initial, indirectly determined, ontogenetic adaptations provide, in effect, a scaffolding that bridges the gap to inherited and evolved direct adaptations.

Whilst certainly not confined just to ontogenetic adaptations produced by learning or other forms of intelligence, for Baldwin the new factor was a means of introducing mind as a force in evolution. He was, as Richards notes, a "spiritualist metaphysician" who "felt the beat of consciousness in the universe." It provided for Baldwin a means of strengthening his monism in which mind did not stand outside of nature.

Organic selection, whilst not Lamarckian, goes some way to explaining the existence of complex coadaptations, any one of which on its own would not produce an adaptive outcome but which collectively do. Again the notion of scaffolding is helpful.

The ontogenetic adaptation holds together a complex of elements across generations giving the necessary time for them to be subsumed by and accommodated into genetically based characteristics. It provided a Darwinian explanation of just those complex adaptations that Lamarckians like Spencer had argued undermined a purely Darwinian explanation. It also put substance and direction on the confused picture that Darwin had left behind as to the relationship between instincts and learning.

Organic selection as a factor in evolution was not dismissed as trivial at the time. Whilst it only became known as the Baldwin Effect in the 1950s it was widely discussed as an important contribution to evolutionary theory at that time. Later evolutionary luminaries like Julian Huxley considered it a real evolutionary force; and George Gaylord Simpson and Ernst Mayr took it seriously enough to criticize it. Baldwin became known beyond the narrow confines of the new science of psychology as a figure of consequence in biology, even if, for the second time, the issue of just how much Baldwin owed the idea to others followed hard on the heels of the first published papers on organic selection. The difficulty arose because at almost exactly the same time, similar ideas were put forward by the paleontologist Henry Fairfield Osborn and the excellent Conway Lloyd Morgan. Osborn was a Lamarckian seeking for a way of reconciling Lamarckian and Darwinian theory. But both Morgan and Baldwin were, by the middle 1890s at least, staunch Darwinians and it is indeed remarkable that at the same meeting of the New York Academy of Sciences, Morgan, who was touring the United States in the winter of 1895–96, gave a paper immediately preceding one by Baldwin, the two men, to the surprise of the audience, presenting almost identical ideas. Richards considers it most likely to be another case of parallel evolution in science, understood in the context of the influence of Romanes on both men. Morgan had just completed editing a posthumous volume of Romanes' writings, and the focus of Baldwin's talk at that New York meeting was precisely that book, in which Romanes, amongst other matters, considered how individual intelligence might shield animals from the effects of natural selection. In general, the buffering effects of ontogenetic adaptations are a constant theme in this corner of evolutionary biology. Given other strong communalities of thought between them – both subscribed to a powerful monism, both recognized the importance of development, both proffered versions of internal selection to account for some forms of intelligence, and both considered human culture to serve a Lamarckian end by a Darwinian means – given such communalities, it is entirely plausible that Romanes served as a spur for both to arrive at the same idea. Morgan himself did not judge it any kind of an issue since he considered that he himself had essentially borrowed the idea from Romanes and Weismann. Baldwin, by contrast, was a hubristic and defensive man, and he consistently published accounts which tended subtly to portray himself as the sole originator of the notion. He also wrote with sufficient frequency upon the topic in the most influential of journals for organic selection later to become known as the Baldwin effect. When a principle or law in science comes to bear a name, the owner of the name wins any argument about origins of formulation. In any event, as with imitation, Baldwin made the idea of organic selection do conceptual work in a way that Morgan did not. For that reason alone the Baldwin effect is aptly named.

In the 1940s and 1950s the British evolutionist and developmentalist C.H. Waddington developed the concept of genetic assimilation, an idea with strong surface similarities to the Baldwin effect. It is significant that Waddington was Piaget's evolutionary guru. It is certainly the case that Waddington has been a key figure in the recent revival of interest in the relationship between development and evolution and the attempted synthesis of ontogeny and phylogeny under the (distressing) label of "evo-devo." For Waddington, the genotypes of most complex multicellular organisms contain greater genetic variability than is expressed in the phenotype, as well as buffered developmental pathways, what he termed canalization, which protect against environmental and intra-genomic perturbation, and ensure the development of relatively fixed phenotypic forms. However, under conditions of considerable stress, like a severe environmental trauma (sudden and significant temperature change, for instance), some of this previously unexpressed genetic variation may find expression in novel phenotypic form, and if selection for the new form occurs, then through canalization the novel phenotypic character will become fixed in expression and occur even in the absence of the initiating environmental event. Waddington was able to point to numerous experimental findings on the structure of fruit flies and other laboratory preparations, as well as field observations (including classic early zoological studies on freshwater snails by Piaget), which supported his arguments for the existence of genetic assimilation.

Waddington's conception, and findings, look very like the Baldwin effect; and cast in modern genetic terminology it is even more clearly not a Lamarckian process because what the environmental event causes to be expressed is already existing genetic variation. And here is the difference from organic selection. For Baldwin, who, remember, conceived his idea in a pre-Mendelian age and hence was quite unable to think of how his new factor might work in the hard currency of real inheritance mechanisms, the changes in whatever constituted those mechanisms, genes, came after the environment had elicited novel adaptations by way of phenotypic plasticity. That is a very important difference which makes Waddington's idea a more plausible and likely evolutionary force than the Baldwin effect. But that does not reduce Baldwin's (and Morgan's) prescience, their sheer cleverness, in offering an addition to Darwin's processes to account for evolutionary change, when they knew nothing whatever about genetics. In that sense, Baldwin was more original than Waddington, which is saying a great deal because Waddington was an evolutionist of creative genius.

There is another resemblance between Waddington and Baldwin. Waddington was a powerful advocate of the view that genetics and natural selection alone provide an insufficient account of how evolution works. He insisted that two other subsystems were as important as the genetic and the selective. These were development and what he termed the exploitive system. The latter operates in animals that "choose" (where to nest, for example, or what to eat), where choice is defined as a specific behavioral act or response amongst a range of possibilities. The choice made is a powerful determinant of selection forces. In this way, psychological mechanisms and processes becoming important determinative events in evolution. Here too is "the beat of consciousness." Baldwin would have wholly approved of Waddington's exploitive system.

About the same time that Waddington was developing his ideas, a Russian evolutionist, one Ivan Ivanovitch Schmalhausen, was writing about autonomization, stabilizing selection, and norms of reaction, all evolutionary processes revolving around the way novel environments might reconfigure development to reveal previously hidden genetic variation. This is obviously very close to Waddington's genetic assimilation, and hence bears some similarity to the Baldwin effect. Then in the 1980s and 1990s the Baldwin effect and genetic assimilation were again used to explain phenomena as diverse as changes from winged to wingless states in some species, and how others effected massive changes in habitat, for instance the shift from life in the sea to living in freshwater, an important part of the history of life on Earth.

Thus it is that Baldwin's name continues to reverberate, if somewhat faintly, amongst contemporary biologists, though the Baldwin effect was, and still is, subject to criticism. The first, which comes from Mayr amongst others, is that the phenotypic plasticity that organic selection requires must itself be an evolved trait. Hence there is nothing new about Baldwin's new factor. This is not a strong point. All it indicates is that evolution has evolved features which facilitate the process of transformation in time. But a complete theory of evolution needs to include these facilitating processes. Just as nobody denies that sexual reproduction evolved, and that sexual reproduction is now a powerful cause of evolutionary transformation, so phenotypic plasticity has evolved, yet is itself a cause of further evolution. It is precisely in the enrichment of evolutionary causes, their pluralism, that the strength of the Baldwin effect, genetic assimilation, and the role of development in evolution (evo-devo) lies. A much more potent criticism of organic selection is this: if phenotypic plasticity leads to adequate adaptations which ensure survival in particular environments, what is the use, indeed what the added value, that would derive from transforming such adaptations already arrived at, albeit it indirectly via evolved mechanisms of plasticity, into those directly put in place by natural selection? If there is no added value, there would be no selective forces to effect the substitution of one source of the adaptation for another.

Baldwin seemed to be aware of this criticism and was never able to answer it. It remains the case, though, that organic selection is a serious contender for a place in a complete theory of evolution, and it is not implausible that an answer will yet be furnished about the plausibility of organic selection as a real force in evolution – perhaps in arguments concerning reliability, or the costs of maintaining information in neural circuits rather than the base-pair sequences of DNA. However this sorts itself out, in even just attracting the attention of evolutionists outside of psychology, Baldwin achieved something that no other psychologist has since managed to do.

Evolutionary Epistemology

The philosopher Karl Popper argued that evolutionary epistemology comes in two forms. The one is centered upon the assumption that intelligence, the ability to gain knowledge (broadly defined and however many different process and mechanisms it encompasses), is, directly or indirectly, a product of evolution. Put in other terms, one cannot take an evolution-free stance in trying to understand how it is we can know anything of the world. The other is the idea that the means by which we and other animals come to have knowledge is the result of processes that are identical to those by which species are transformed in time. The former is a commonplace belief held by every scientist, though there are a wide range of subsidiary assumptions that can, and are, called upon which results in rather different theoretical stances. It is only in recent years that this has become an issue of real importance and the whole matter of knowledge as product of evolution will be returned to in chapter 7. The notion that knowledge is gained by way of the same processes that the evolution of species occurs, in contrast, is a much more controversial claim subscribed to by a comparatively small number of psychologists and philosophers. If correct, it is the closest thing there is in biology to a unified theory equivalent to quantum mechanics and relativity in physics.

The relationship between these two forms of evolutionary epistemology is not simple. For one thing, subscribing to the belief that all forms of intelligence are products of evolution does not entail the belief that all forms of intelligence are driven by the same set of processes by which they came into existence. In other words, it does not logically follow that evolution as a process of transformation could only give rise to other forms of transformation identical in process to itself. Thus one can be an evolutionary epistemologist of the first kind without being the second sort. Furthermore, if knowledge gain and change is caused by the same set of processes that drive all forms of change in biological systems, this does not mean that the ability to know, intelligence of any kind, was bound to have evolved in some organisms. It merely asserts that when it has evolved, it has always taken a certain form. There is also a possible intermediate position. This is to subscribe to the view that some, but not necessarily all, forms of knowledge gain are driven by the same processes that Darwin discovered.

So there is an asymmetry here. Creationists and believers in miracles aside, we are all evolutionary epistemologists of the first kind. A not insubstantial number of psychologists adopt the intermediate stance. But few are evolutionary epistemologists through and through by believing all forms of knowledge gain are identical as processes to that of evolution.

Baldwin, like Morgan, was close to being an evolutionary epistemologist through and through. In *Darwin and the Humanities* he wrote:

> The problem of "educability", of "profiting by experience", has been attacked throughout the entire range of organic forms, with striking harmony of results, summed up by the phrase "trial and error". From the infusoria's limited modification of behavior to the child's extended education, it is found that all learning is by a process of strenuous, excessive, and varied discharges. Through such discharges adjustive modifications occur ... It takes place in a manner to which the Darwinian conception of selection is strictly applicable. (Baldwin, 1909, p. 16)

Both Baldwin and Morgan also extended the reach of universal Darwinian processes into the social realm, with both men following Wallace, perhaps the earliest evolutionary epistemologist of a Darwinian cast, in believing that cultural change proceeds in exactly the same way as does species' change. Spencer, of course (see chapter 2), had also done so and before anyone else, but he had backed the wrong evolutionary theory.

Wallace had extended the idea of the evolutionary processes, that he had discovered along with Darwin, into culture in the middle 1860s. In both cases, whether species' evolution or cultural change, evolution was envisaged as a set of processes operating between individuals. Just a few years later, T.H. Huxley, Darwin's great friend and defender, played with the idea that evolution of a Darwinian kind occurs **within** individuals:

It is a probable hypothesis that what the world is to organisms in general, each organism is to the molecules of which it is composed. Multitudes of these, having diverse tendencies, are competing with one another for opportunity to exist and multiply; and the organism as a whole is as much the product of the molecules which are victorious as the Fauna and Flora of a country are the product of the glorious organic beings in it. (In Oppenheim, 1982, p. 28)

It is odd that Darwin wrote to his friend saying "I am very glad that you have been bold enough to give your idea about Natural Selection among the molecules, though I cannot quite follow you," because at this very time Darwin was working on the *Descent of Man*. In chapter 3 of that book, whilst considering language, Darwin musing upon the parallels between the formation of different languages and of species wrote that "the survival or preservation of certain favored words in the struggle for existence is natural selection." This is as explicit an extension of the evolutionary processes into a realm different from speciation as one can find. Perhaps what Darwin was balking at in Huxley's writing was the within-organism nature of the extension because language change, as he argued for it, occurred as a between-individual phenomenon. Further application of Darwinian natural selection to individual development was made by the developmentalist W. Roux, the very title of whose 1881 book *Der Kampf der Theile in Organismus* (The Struggle of the Parts in the Organism) is redolent of Darwin's theory. In 1894 Weismann delivered the Romanes lecture at Oxford in which he put forward the notion of "intra-selection," which likely strongly influenced Morgan and Baldwin. And so the circle closes. William James actually preceded both in terms of placing variation and selection as processes in the mind with an article in the October 1880 issue of the *Atlantic Monthly*. This essay, vehemently anti-Spencer, was an analysis of creative thought in terms of an internalizing of Darwin's theory:

> new conceptions, emotions and active tendencies which evolve are originally **produced** in the shape of random images, fancies, accidental outbirths of spontaneous variation in the functional activity of the excessively unstable human brain, which the outer environment simply confirms or refutes, adopts or rejects, preserves or destroys, – **selects**, in short, just as it selects morphological and

social variations due to molecular accidents of an analogous sort.
(James, 1880, p. 456; original emphasis)

For reasons that will be explained in the next section of this chapter, Baldwin's influence became particularly strong in France after about 1910 and correspondingly reduced in north America. The French Swiss developmentalist Jean Piaget, raised within an intellectual environment in which French ideas would have obviously been predominant, and who created a system of thought about cognitive development of great prominence and significance which he called genetic epistemology, was a major figure in the intellectual lineage linking the processes of knowledge gain with evolution. Piaget, in fact, in a 1979 interview, was dismissive of Baldwin's influence on his own ideas. "The global idea of genesis. That's what's important to me" was all that he would own to when asked what part of Baldwin's work he considered important. Piaget's stages of cognitive development in the growing child, the central role of equilibration by which, through the processes of assimilation and accommodation, the actions of the organism (he considers his theory to have a generality way beyond that of just human cognition) achieve a relationship of balance with a changing world, are set within a very different conceptual framework to the main line of evolutionary epistemology centered upon Darwin's processes of variation, selection, and the conservation and transmission of selected variants. Piaget was deeply skeptical of the idea that chance variation plays a significant role in evolution, and disliked what he considered to be the essential passivity of individual organisms in the evolutionary process. Piaget's views stemmed from his structuralist conceptions of complex organization, self-regulation, coordination, and construction, rather than variation and selection. Nonetheless he ran a strong line on adaptive organization as the linking relationship between evolution and cognition. For some 50 years Piaget was a major contributor, if a somewhat wayward one, to the central idea that there are common processes to the way evolution and cognition work. Towards the end of his life Piaget wrote several books directly addressing these theoretical issues. They edged ever closer to a Lamarckianism, and eventually Piaget seemed to fall over that edge. His intolerance of Darwinian evolution left him rather isolated when evolutionary epistemology flowered, though it was but a small bloom, from the 1960s onwards.

There were three reasons why evolutionary epistemology regained some prominence. The first was the rising interest, explained in subsequent chapters, in placing psychology once again within an evolutionary framework, a framework that had been largely absent since the 1920s. The second were changes of thinking in immunology in the late 1950s and 1960s. Under the principal theoretical influences of F.M. Burnet in Australia and N.K. Jerne in Europe, which were supported by the rapid advances in molecular biology, immune system function came to be understood in an entirely different light. Whereas previously it was thought to operate as an instructionalist system (see chapter 3), within a short time this was replaced by the view that central to immune system function are the processes of variation and selection. If the immune system is a Darwin machine that constantly adapts the internal chemistry of the body to unforeseeable encounters with the microorganisms that assail us, then why should we not try to understand the brain and cognition as a similar kind of device, or set of devices, that operate in the same way to allow adaptation to unpredictable physical and social encounters?

The third was the tireless proselytizing of Donald Campbell. Campbell was an eminent social psychologist with a strong interest in philosophy and evolutionary theory. From the late 1950s he began to publish accounts of perception, intelligence, and cultural change from the perspective of a blind-variation-and-selective-retention epistemology, a thorough-going Darwinian account of knowledge gain and growth. With an encyclopedic knowledge of the history of evolutionary epistemology he built upon the work of all those previously mentioned, including Baldwin, of course, as well as the physicist Ernst Mach, Konrad Lorenz (see next chapter), the cybernetician Ross Ashby, and preeminently Popper. Others who contributed to this rising tide of opinion that a selectionist view of knowledge gain has conceptual force were B.F.Skinner, the Nobel Laureat H.A. Simon, the philosopher Daniel Dennett, and Richard Dawkins who coined the phrase universal Darwinism.

We are too close to the present to make a judgment as to whether evolutionary epistemology in the form of selection theory will lead to significant discoveries. A 40-fold rise in publications on the topic since 1974, the year which saw a seminal paper by Campbell, when compared with previous years, tells us little about the actual conceptual power of the idea. There has certainly been a rash of discoveries about developmental processes, **and mechanisms**, which point to the scope of selectionist theory. Gerald Edelman, another Nobel prize winner, has vigorously propagated this approach for the development of the nervous system. However, selection theory is often dismissed, as it was by Noam Chomsky in 1982, as a vague analogy which signifies nothing.

Two things are needed if the Baldwinian version of evolutionary epistemology is to deliver as serious science in the future. One is that just as Darwin's theory was transformed as science by the marriage of his processes to the mechanisms of genetics, so what is now needed are get-at-able, put-your-finger-on psychological and neurochemical mechanisms that will do the same job for the proposed epistemological processes. Edelman's work is the way and the light, not analyses in words which seek to substitute instructional processes with those that are selective. The second is to acknowledge the breadth of selection theory by a theoretical structure of appropriately grand scope. If we and other animals come to have knowledge by way of the same processes that result in adaptation, speciation, development, and immune system function, but driven by different mechanisms, then we badly need a defensible architecture of complexity that binds them all into a coherent conceptual structure.

Fall and Decline

In the summer of 1908 Baldwin was caught in a police raid on a brothel in Baltimore. Although he was discovered to have initially given a false name, the charges were dropped. However, some months later the police report somehow found its way into the hands of the Chair of the John Hopkins University board of trustees. Baldwin's life as an American academic was at an end. What was thought to be even more scandalous than a senior scholar being found in a brothel (though why he was there and what he was doing was never clearly established) was that the prostitutes were black. Baldwin resigned his job and took up a temporary post in Mexico. A year later he and his family moved to France where he lived in Paris until he died.

The French were not the least scandalized. He had much contact with the likes of Emile Boutroux, Henri Bergson, Henri Poincaré, Pierre Janet, and Edouard Claparade, amongst others. These were amongst the most influential philosophers, mathematicians, and psychologists in France at that time. Perhaps of especial significance were Claparade and Janet, the former being one of Piaget's mentors in Geneva and the latter his teacher in Paris. Vygotsky in Russia also read and admired Baldwin's work. So Baldwin's influence remained in Europe. It did not do so in north America for several reasons.

Hypocrisy and moral outrage were strong social forces in the north America of 1909. Baldwin, and by strong association his ideas, had become tainted and this distaste undoubtedly had an effect on how people viewed his ideas and the reduced frequency with which they were discussed. It is also the case that Baldwin, who as editor of the *Psychological Review* (which he resigned along with his Hopkins post), Chair of a number of important committees overseeing psychological science in the United States, and as President of many influential conferences and congresses, plummeted from being one of the most prominent and conspicuous presences in American psychology to a near total absence. There were no continuing generations of students passing his word along, and former colleagues didn't want to talk of him or his ideas. In science you **are** your ideas. Finally, Baldwin's resignation led to the inexorable rise of Watson who while he inherited both Baldwin's job at John Hopkins and his editorship of the *Psychological Review* would have no truck with theory, Baldwin's or anyone else's.

Baldwin must have loathed behaviorism which stood for nothing that his psychology was based on. In his autobiographical notes written late in his life he considers it to be biology and is explicit in rejecting it as psychology. But in those days Europe was a long way from America and Baldwin became increasingly a philosopher. As for American psychology it was, for the time being, done with European ideas, and done with evolutionary theory. It would be over 50 years before psychologists would begin again to think that evolutionary biology had something to say to their discipline.

CHAPTER SIX

Lessons to be Learned:
Ethology and Sociobiology

Instinct theory was revived in the middle of the twentieth century by the rise of a branch of zoology called ethology. Ethology rose rapidly to real scientific prominence, three ethologists in 1973 being awarded the first ever Nobel Prize for studies of behavior. But by the late 1970s ethology had diminished in importance as sociobiology came even more quickly to dominate the evolutionary study of behavior. Neither ethology nor sociobiology had their origins in any intention to revive evolutionary accounts of human behavior. In other words, neither ethologists nor sociobiologists considered themselves a part of psychology – quite the reverse, each was inclined to argue that human psychology is a special case of these more encompassing sciences – and neither ethologists nor sociobiologists were considered by most psychologists to have much to do with their discipline. However, both were conceptually powerful disciplines in their own right, and both gained that power by being exemplars of the principle of specific application. That is, specific aspects of evolutionary theory drove both empirical studies and causal explanations. Because of their prominence, arising in part from the controversy each generated, both laid the foundations for the resurgence of evolutionary thinking in psychology itself in the 1980s and 1990s. As practitioners of the principle of specific application, both had lessons in science for what was to come. They also taught lessons on the misuse of science that were not always heeded.

Classical Ethology

One reason for the collapse of the notion of instincts in psychology in the early part of the twentieth century was that it was so conceptually weak, if not entirely empty (chapter 4). Part of that weakness was a result of hopeless inconsistencies in the way different people thought of the problem. One strong line of thought, which begins with Greek philosophers half a millennium before the birth of Christ, is that whilst humans are rational and conscious beings, beasts are not and their behavior is entirely inborn. This became consistent with subsequent Christian teaching according to which it is only humans who have an afterlife and whose fate therein depends upon our ability to distinguish with our intellects between right and wrong. Reason is in the service of moral choices that other animals do not have to make. Descartes' beast machine (chapter 2) which cannot think and has no language drew the same distinction between ourselves and all other animals. Instincts, it was held, owed nothing to experience, where experience was framed within the concept of rational powers of learning and reasoning. The sensationalists adopted an almost opposite view. By way of their empiricist origins they were reluctant to accept the existence of instincts in humans, and when they did they laid emphasis on these being acquired and not inborn. Lamarck, and hence Spencer too, in an odd way reconciled these opposing positions by arguing that instincts are the acquired habits of previous generations. Darwin's partial acceptance of the Lamarckian inheritance of acquired characters resulted in his own, uncharacteristic, inconsistency as to just what the relationship between intelligence and instinct is (chapter 3). Romanes' own Lamarckianism led him to believe that instincts are modifiable and learned habits their precursors, whilst Morgan's minimalist conception of innate behaviors as the foundations upon which played powerful (and general) learning processes contrasted sharply with Galton whose overweening hereditarianism reduced all psychological traits to instincts. This was all, put bluntly, a conceptual stew.

Only one thing stood out with any clarity. This was Darwin's 1859 insistence (in contrast to the confusion of the 1871 book) that, whatever their evolutionary origins, for the **individual** animal (including humans), instincts do not originate in prior experience, are without conscious purpose, and are as important to individual survival as corporeal structures and hence are products of evolution. These were the core assumptions upon which ethology was established in the 1930s, with Konrad Lorenz (1903–89) its undisputed conceptual father.

Ethology, as the study of animals in their natural habitat, in contrast to their investigation, dead (more usually) or alive, within the laboratory, is a word that originates in nineteenth-century French biology (though that is certainly not its original usage). The German biologist, Oskar Heinroth, whose influence on Lorenz was exceptional, used the word to distinguish the study of behavior in natural environments from laboratory work. Lorenz's publications by and large do not use the word much, and not at all in his early journal articles. But the word came to stick, in precisely the way Heinroth meant, and so eventually labeled an entire approach to the study of behavior.

Ethology has its earliest beginnings in the observations of eighteenth-century naturalists like van Pernau, Réaumur, and Reimarus, as well as Spalding and Fabré of the nineteenth century, who were describing complex but seemingly fixed and stereotyped behaviors common to all members of a species, often enough of invertebrates. Jacob van Uexkull and Jacques Loeb provided essential elements, as did Charles Otis Whitman and his student Wallace Craig. Heinroth cannot be left out of any account. What is striking about such a list is that none of them were psychologists. All were naturalists or trained zoologists. However, it was Lorenz who drew everything together and created ethology as a separate science.

Lorenz's father was a successful and wealthy orthopedic surgeon who had, before Lorenz's birth, developed an estate at Altenberg, north of Vienna. From an early age Lorenz adored animals of every kind, especially birds and fish, though rabbits, dogs, cats, and monkeys were also a part of the vivid world he created for himself. The estate provided an ideal situation for the long hours spent as a child collecting, nurturing, and observing these creatures. At high school he was taught evolution by a Benedictine monk and he was actively encouraged in his zoological interests. As Lorenz notes in his autobiographical sketch: "On finishing high school I was still obsessed with evolution and wanted to study zoology and palaeontology," but he bent to his father's wishes that he study medicine, which he did at Columbia

University in New York and in Vienna. He graduated with a medical degree in 1928 and was awarded a Ph.D. in zoology five years later. Whilst studying medicine he was taught comparative anatomy by Ferdinand Hochstetter and attended the psychology seminars of Karl Buhler. His passion for pursuing the study of animal behavior in its natural setting was well established when he began to read the writings of psychologists (he specifically picks out McDougall and Watson). But, in his view, "none of these people *knew* animals, none of them was an expert." Then his great friend Bernard Hellman gave him a copy of one of Heinroth's books and "I realized in a flash that this man knew everything about behavior.... that I had believed to be the only one to know. Here, at last, was a scientist who was also an expert."

Lorenz's ideas derived from three core convictions. The first is that certain elements of behavior are products of evolution that can only be understood by its study within the environment in which it evolved, what evolutionary psychologists 50 years later would call the environment of evolutionary adaptiveness. In his most famous early paper of 1935, *Der Kumpan in der Umwelt des Vogels* (Companionship in Bird Life) he wrote that "unless we know the natural behavior of a species, experiments are largely worthless." The second was that this necessity, the knowledge of behavior as it occurred in natural environments, is rooted in behavior's adaptive functions which must be at least partly genetically caused. These behaviors he considered to be instincts. The third core idea was that instincts could be most fruitfully understood and analyzed within a strict phylogenetically based comparative framework. This framework is homology, which means similarity of a trait as a result of common ancestry. Thus, if two species, B and C, possess traits Y and Z which display certain criteria of similarity, such traits are homologous if it can be shown that some species, A, existed, ancestral to B and C, which possessed a trait X which was the forerunner to traits Y and Z. Here then was a program for studying and understanding behavior within a framework of very specific evolutionary application. As Lorenz freely and frequently acknowledged, this was a position straight out of Whitman's dictum that "instincts and organs are to be studied from the common viewpoint of phyletic descent."

Lorenz's original conception was that instincts were based on chains of reflexes, but discussion with Erich von Holst, with whom he was later to establish a Max Planck Institute for the study of the physiology of behavior, persuaded him that the reflex idea was wrong. Instead he moved to the less specific notion of a more complex central nervous system unit whose activity is released by some sensory event, a sign stimulus or releaser, which triggers an "innate releasing mechanism" that allows the sequence of behavior, a "fixed action pattern," to be run off "at the biologically 'right' moment." In the *Kumpan* paper Lorenz took a strong stand which was to characterize much of his thinking. "It is my belief" he wrote "that instinctive reactions are basically different from all other types of behavior . . . that there is no homology between instinctive actions and all acquired or insightful behavior."

Amongst many, the *Kumpan* paper made three other important points. One was that social stimuli in the form of the behavior of conspecifics, are important innate releasing mechanisms in the instinctive interactions between social species. Another was that "it is hardly possible to point out a more impressive feature of instinctive actions than their property to 'go off *in vacuo*' when the specific releasing stimuli are absent." Such vacuum activity led him to a kind of hydraulic model for the motivation and generation of instincts. The third concerned domestication. "The laws that govern the behavior of domestic species are superseded and, to a great extent, neutralized by others of an entirely different nature. This competition of two totally diverse principles, one of which borders on pathology, results, if not in chaos, at any rate in a state of great confusion." His concerns about the effects of domestication on instinctive behavior were later to lead him into political difficulties.

In 1936 Lorenz attended a symposium on instincts in Holland, and there he met Nikolaas (Niko) Tinbergen (1907–88). They formed an immediate and long-lasting friendship. Lorenz invited Tinbergen to Altenberg where they began a famous collaboration. In his autobiographical notes, Tinbergen wrote of how "Konrad's extraordinary vision and enthusiasm were supplemented and fertilised by my critical sense, my inclination to think his ideas through, and my irrepressible urge to check our 'hunches' by experimentation – a gift for which he had an almost childish admiration. Throughout this we often burst into bouts of hilarious fun – in Konrad's words, in *Lausbuberei*." One result was a classic coauthored paper on a series of observations and experiments on egg-retrieval in the greylag goose, which further developed the concept of instinct by adding in the important notion of taxes or taxis compounds as the means by which instinctive acts are oriented and guided.

Tinbergen, whose *The Study of Instinct* published in 1951 was the first textbook on ethology, had also as a young boy been fascinated by the behavior of animals. He had kept stickleback fish in an open-air aquarium and closely observed their courtship and mating. As an ethologist he was to publish influential papers on this topic, in which he described the coordinated interactions between male and female fish as each served, in their anatomy or behavior, as an innate releaser for the instinctive behavior of the other, the result being an intricate chain of coupled instincts as the male leads the female to its nest where the eggs are laid and fertilized. Tinbergen studied biology as a student and was much influenced by the writings on invertebrate behavior by Fabré and by another major German zoologist, Karl von Frisch (1886–1982), who achieved fame through his experiments on honey bees which demonstrated how foragers returning to the hive signaled the position of food sources to other bees in the hive by "dancing." Conscientious, affable, and open-minded, Tinbergen was awarded in 1938 a free passage to the United States where he lectured and met important evolutionists, biologists, and psychologists like Mayr, Yerkes, and, significantly, T.C. Schneirla, who was later to be a fierce critic of classical ethology. "I was frankly bewildered by what I saw of American psychology" he noted. He returned to Holland in the immediate aftermath of the Munich crisis and a year later Europe was engulfed by World War Two.

Not long before the outbreak of the war, Lorenz had been appointed to the Chair of Psychology at the Albertus University of Konigsberg in eastern Prussia. (It was well understood that Lorenz was no psychologist, but they had really wanted someone who combined a knowledge of biology with an interest in Kant's epistemology, and Lorenz fitted that role and had powerful friends at the university.) But that was a post that did not last for long. Drafted into the army, Lorenz served as a medical officer, first in a psychiatric clinic and later as a field surgeon on the eastern front. He was captured by Soviet forces at Vitebsk in 1944 and sent to prisoner-of-war camps, first in Soviet Armenia and later close to Moscow. He was well treated by his own account and despite his continuing medical role, found time to write epistemology. Finally released in 1947 he returned to Altenberg in early 1948.

His friend and colleague Tinbergen had had a very different war. Arrested by the occupying Germans because of his protests at the dismissal of Jewish academics from Dutch universities he was imprisoned in a hostage camp in Germany for two years. On release he returned to Holland and worked in the Dutch Resistance. Despite these very different experiences, when Lorenz and Tinbergen met again in England in 1949, they were able to resume their friendship. It was some years before each settled back into normal academic life, Tinbergen in England and Lorenz at various posts in Germany and Austria.

After 1950 ethology, which in the 1930s was largely unknown outside of mainland Europe, began to spread, especially in the English-speaking world. As it did so, ethology expanded, especially empirically, the latter in no small part because of Tinbergen's influence. Observation studies of, for example, gulls with a detail and extent of recording that was unprecedented, and correspondingly revealing, were carried out. It became clear that animals had to be observed over much longer periods than had occurred previously if their behavior were to be truly and completely documented. The coordinated predatory behavior of chimpanzees, for example, discovered much later when ethological methodology was exported to Africa, would likely never have been recorded by the kind of casual observation previous generations of naturalists had indulged in. Convinced by Lorenz's arguments on the importance of systematic comparative work, the behavior of ground-nesting gulls (which is much the most common form) and cliff-nesters like kittiwakes were compared in great detail, the differences observed ascribed to differences in the ecological demands of ground versus cliff nesting. Tinbergen also continued to pioneer field experiments. Intrigued by differences between a ground-nesting black-headed gulls and kittiwakes in terms of egg-shell removal after chicks are hatched, it was shown in a classic series of experiments, by replacing broken shells in the nests and counting the incidence of nest raiding by overflying predators, that the nest cleaning behavior of the black-headed gull was an important group of behaviors that reduced predation rates and significantly improved individual survival. Kittiwakes are messy nesters because there are no predatory pressures in their cliff-nesting sites.

Post-war ethologists also increased basic theoretical ideas. Notions of the hierarchical organization of motivational and goal states were developed, in part in response to empirical observations of phenomena like displacement activities, where a seemingly inappropriate behavior is shown by, for instance, fighting cocks who will break off their aggressive interaction to peck at the ground as if feeding, or to preen themselves. The argument was that the displacement activity occurred when the activities higher in the hierarchy of actions and their associated drives become inhibited, thus allowing lower-level activities to appear. Ethologists also built on Julian Huxley's 1920s idea of ritualized behaviors, whereby fragments of fixed action patterns change by processes of exaggeration, formalization, and repetition to become important within-species forms of communication, which in the case of aggression, by increasing the amount of "posing" allied to physical characters like body bulk or horn size, might serve to reduce physical injury arising from agonistic interactions.

As ethology grew, so too, of course, did the criticisms. The principal source of these was Lorenz's hard stand on the need absolutely to separate learned from instinctive behavior. Everybody acknowledged that complex sequences of behavior are of mixed provenance. But whereas his critics argued that each element making up the sequence was a consequence of the interaction of different causes, genetics and learning included, for Lorenz each element had a single cause, and those that were a product of evolution, were pure and unadulterated instincts.

Imprinting was a case in point. In the nineteenth century, Spalding in England had noted that "chickens, as soon as they are able to walk, will follow any moving object. And, when guided by sight alone, they seem to have no more disposition to follow a hen than to follow a duck, or a human being." Following some elementary experiments Spalding observed that the following response was determined at least in part by age because beyond a certain time after hatching "they ran from me instead of to me." William James set the stage for viewing imprinting in instinct terms by writing that Spalding had shown the action of "opposite instincts of attachment and fear." Heinroth had been much struck by young birds becoming attached to so incongruous a figure as a human, but it was Lorenz, in his popular writing, who made the phenomenon famous with the photographic image of himself being followed by a line of duck-lings. In his early characterization of imprinting Lorenz was adamant that learning of any kind did not determine the following behavior, that it is an instinctive response, irreversible, and temporally bound to specific physiological states in the imprinted animals. A great deal of experimental work subse-quently showed that only the last of his assertions is correct and he had to give way to the evidence. But imprinting typified the criticism of his basic position on instinct that began in the 1950s from, amongst others, Donald Hebb, T.C. Schneirla, Robert Hinde, and, notably, Daniel Lehrman whose "A critique of Kon-rad Lorenz's theory of instinctive behavior" of 1953 remains a seminal critical analysis of classical ethology's conception of instinct.

These attacks, and the word attack is used advisedly because over the period beginning in the early 1950s and extending well into the 1960s the exchanges were heated and not a little per-sonal, were multipronged and powerful. Only two major points need concern us here. The first was that Lorenz's absolute dis-tinction between instincts and learned behaviors, between the innate and the acquired, is a false dichotomy. The second, which followed from the first, was that the dichotomy left out of any causal analysis of behavior the importance of develop-ment. Empirical cases refuting Lorenz's position came thick and fast. For example, in an extensive series of observations and experiments on the feeding behavior of sea gull chicks by Jack Hailman, the American ethologist (the term quickly came to have wider reference to the study of animal behavior in the wild in Britain and the United States, regardless of adherence, or lack of it, to the Lorenzian view of instincts), the thesis of pure determin-ation of behavioral elements as either instinctive or learned was shown to be untenable. Within days of hatching, adult gulls lower their heads and point their beaks down in front of the chick. The latter aims a coordinated pecking motion at the parent's bill which it then grasps and strokes with a downward motion. After repeated pecking, grasping, and stroking the adult bird regurgitates some food which the chick then eats. Hailman showed conclusively that such begging behavior by the chick is not fully formed after hatching but instead each element in the begging sequence changes during development, elements such as the positioning of the chick relative to the adult altering, and the accuracy of the peck improving, with practice. What made Hailman's work so persuasive was the detailed dissection of a seemingly simple behavior into its constituent elements, and so provided a real test for the fundamental difference between Lorenz and his critics – is any element of a behavioral sequence determined by a single cause? One surprising feature of Hailman's findings was that despite striking differences in appearance between herring gull and laughing gull adults, the chicks do not show differences in their responsiveness to adults of their own or the other species. He also showed marked effects of chicks reared in isolation, or in the company of another chick who might be naive or experienced at begging for food. This strongly suggests some form of social learning. The overall finding was that neither this behavior as a complex sequence, nor any of its constituent elements, so important to the survival of these young birds, could be described simply and purely as innate and instinctive in origin.

An equally striking example was the observation by the American psychologist Harry Harlow of pathologically impaired sexual behavior in monkeys reared in social isolation. But monkeys do not learn through early social interactions with conspecifics appropriate sexual behavior when very young animals, behavior which at least intuitively might be thought of as instinctive and which only becomes manifest years later. Other causal factors are operating here, factors rooted in experience which powerfully influences the development of behavior. The extreme example of developmental effects is the biasing of receptive fields of cells in the visual cortex of animals reared seeing either only horizontal or vertical striations during early life. No animal learns to orientate its cortical visual fields. Factors other than learning or instinct are at work.

The responses of the founding fathers of ethology to such criticisms and findings were somewhat different. Tinbergen developed a much more inclusive approach to ethology. Lorenz was forced to a profound insight. In 1963 Tinbergen's "On the aims and methods of Ethology" published in English in the *Zeitschrift fur Tierpsychologie* built on Huxley's analysis of the major divisions of study within biology and argued for ethology as a discipline conceptually arrayed around four major questions. These are what he called, somewhat confusingly, causation (by which he meant the proximate physiological and anatomical bases of species-specific behaviors), survival value (referring to the adaptedness of such behavior and hence the reason why it evolved), ontogeny (the study of how species-specific behaviors develop in individuals) and evolution (the relationship between similar behaviors in different species, or its phylogeny). Tinbergen's "four whys," as they came to be widely called, signaled a rapprochement between the classical formulation of ethology and its then contemporary critics and practitioners. Lorenz is omnipresent in that paper, but so too are Lehrman, Hinde, and others who had taken up arms in the 1950s against the concept of any behavior as purely innate and instinctive.

Lorenz took a rather different tack. In 1965 he published a monograph entitled *Evolution and Modification of Behavior*. In it he attempted to retrieve his notion of the innate by conceding that if behavior cannot be innate in his original sense of purely genetically caused, the information that underlies the adaptiveness of behavior is innate. These are words that merely restate his assumption of the importance of genes. However, what was groundbreaking was the stance he took on the supposed dichotomy between what is innate and what is learned. Long interested in epistemology, Lorenz was a Kantian, and the most prominent feature of Kant's epistemology were the *a priori* intuitions and categories. For some decades Lorenz had been moving towards seeing epistemological *a prioris* as evolved cognitive capacities and in the 1965 monograph he explicitly adopted this position to defend himself against the charge that he dealt in indefensible dichotomies. "The amazing and never-to-be-forgotten fact is that learning does, in the majority of cases, increase the survival value of the behavior mechanisms which it modifies." If learning is almost always adaptive in outcome, then learning itself must be an evolved trait – learning is an instinct, and so there is no possibility of dichotomous thinking. All behavior modification, whether it be a product of plastic developmental processes or learning, collapses into the singularity of evolved modifiability. This was a brilliant conceptual move with very specific implications which almost all biologists with an interest in learning today take for granted. Lorenz suggested that all intelligent animals have evolved "innate teaching mechanisms" (which he sometimes referred to as innate schoolmarms) that guide and constrain learning. The notion that learning is innately constrained, that nurture has nature, originated solely with Lorenz, and it is all the more impressive in that his claim that learning is almost always adaptive in outcome was sheer hubris based upon the certainty that his argument had to be correct. There was no evidence at the time to support his assertion. Almost all learning theorists in psychology were firm in their belief in the opposite, in general and unconstrained learning processes and mechanisms. No-one conceived of learning as a set of evolved and different processes and mechanisms. It was only after 1965 that evidence of constraints on learning began to accumulate and by then Lorenz was being given little credit for anything.

Lorenz had already antagonized many social scientists with his 1963 book *On Aggression*. He had written two popular books in the 1950s on animal behavior, some of which contained passing reference to humans. *On Aggression* was a different matter. It was not meant to have the charm of his earlier *King Solomon's Ring*. Instead it was a bleakly pessimistic book which argued for aggression as an instinct common to many animals, but that humans are uniquely murderous in having lost the ritualistic displays that in most other species reduces the actual physical damage of aggressive interactions. He also implied that human warfare results from our aggressive instinct. "I think we must face the fact that militant enthusiasm has evolved from the hackle-raising and chin-protruding communal defense instinct of our pre-human ancestors." Most social scientists, and all historians of war, rightly considered this to be errant nonsense. But the range of criticisms, and their impact which eventually resulted in one of the United Nations bodies, UNESCO, officially endorsing the rebuttal to Lorenz called "The Seville Statement on Violence," were not the common fate of other ethologists applying ethological concepts to humans.

Tinbergen himself, so closely allied with Lorenz, had written at some length on early childhood autism, using concepts (and illustrations) drawn from his work on pair-bonding and motivational conflict in herring gulls. The English psychoanalyst John Bowlby was much influenced by Robert Hinde's and other ethologists' accounts of attachment behavior between newly born mammals and their mothers, which he applied virtually unchanged to account for the development of human personality and emotion. Hinde himself went on to write extensively on the biological bases of human social behavior not only to much applause but considered by many to be the exemplar of how properly to extrapolate from the animal behavior literature to the human sciences. Lorenz's close associate Irenaus Eibl-Eibesfeldt wrote a text on human ethology. Nobody complained. There was something about Lorenz that made people uneasy, and that something lay in his very serious concerns about what he considered to be the principal effects of domestication, and what this had led him to do back in the early years of World War Two.

Earlier it was noted that in his *Kumpan* paper Lorenz had already shown an interest in, and anxiety about, the effects of domestication on the behavior of animals. That domestication should lead to changes in behavior is almost a tautology. Domestication is a process of selection primarily for behavioral characteristics which makes a species most tractable to the demands of our own. Domestication sets out to enhance certain behavioral traits like docility and to reduce or eliminate others such as aggression. But Lorenz's concerns were not with those behavioral features that animal breeders specifically select for, and more with incidental side-effects relating to feeding and sexual activity. Domestication, he believed, often, perhaps always, results in the selection of genes that weaken the specificty of innate releasers resulting in indiscriminate appetites for both food and sex. The result, in his view, were animals degenerate in physical characteristics and displaying undesirable behaviors. It was an aesthetic judgment. Again, whilst one might dispute the assumed absolute genetic determination implicit in Lorenz's position, in general few would argue that domestication aims to result in animals that are easy to breed and which consume much food of little interest to humans resulting in larger yields of food that we desire. Lorenz returned to this theme again and again, both before and after the war, and there seems nothing controversial about the matter. However, he took the argument further by equating the effects of domestication in animals with those of "civilization" in humans. This is, at the very least, questionable. Indeed, insofar as domestication involves strong artificial selection for specific characteristics of a species whereas "civilization" results in the diminishing of the effects of natural selection by furnishing adequate nutrition, protection against the elements, and the increased survival of the frail and ill through the agency of applied science, domestication, and "civilization" are completely opposite processes. The only possible connection is that each might be judged to give rise to "degenerates," though by entirely different routes. However, words like degenerates and "undesirables" raises the specter of eugenics, the social Darwinism of the 1920s and racial "theory" of the likes of Haeckel and Davenport (chapter 4). Link that to the Nazis with their own demented form of social Darwinism (they did not like the idea that humans evolved from apes) and the result is as poisonous as one can get. That is what Lorenz did.

In a paper published in 1940 entitled *Durch Domestikation verursachte Storungen arteigenem Verhaltens* (Disorders Caused by the Domestication of Species-specific Behaviour) Lorenz wrote:

> our species-specific sensitivity to the beauty and ugliness of members of our species is intimately connected with the symptoms of degeneration, caused by domestication, which threaten our race ... Usually, a man of high value is disgusted with special intensity by slight symptoms of degeneracy in men of the other race ... In certain circumstances, however, we find not only a lack of this selectivity ... but even a reversal to being attracted by symptoms of degeneracy ... The immensely high reproduction rate in the moral imbecile has long been established ... This phenomenon leads everywhere to the fact that socially inferior human material is enabled to penetrate and finally to annihilate the healthy nation.. The selection for toughness, heroism, social utility ... must be accomplished by some human institution if mankind, in default of selective factors, is not to be ruined by domestication-induced degeneracy. The racial idea as the basis of our state has already accomplished much in this respect ... We must – and should – rely on the healthy feelings of our Best and charge them with the selection which will determine the prosperity or the decay of our people. (In Eisenberg, 1973, p. 124)

This quotation is a translation from a paper by Leon Eisenberg which appeared in *Science* in 1973, the year the Nobel Prize in medicine was awarded jointly to Lorenz, Tinbergen, and von Frisch "for their discoveries concerning organization and elicitation of individual and social behavior patterns." There is, apparently, a mistranslation, according to Alec Nisbett, Lorenz's biographer: "symptoms of degeneracy in people of the other race" should have read "symptoms of degeneracy in people of the other sex." That doesn't alter the tone of Lorenz's piece which identifies him and his ideas closely with Nazi ideology. Nisbett notes that "there was, in fact, more Nazi terminology in the original than Eisenberg had realized."

It is difficult to know quite what to make of this. Lorenz did not write again in that way. His best childhood friend, Bernard Hellman who was Jewish, was believed by Lorenz to have been murdered in one of the death camps. In his autobiographical notes he wrote of the notorious domestication paper thus:

> I was frightened – as I still am – by the thought that analogous genetical processes of deterioration may be at work with civilized humanity. Moved by this fear, I did a very ill-advised thing soon after the Germans had invaded Austria: I wrote about the dangers of domestication and, in order to be understood, I couched my writing in the worst of nazi-terminology. I do not want to extenuate this action. I did, indeed, believe that some good might come of the new rulers. The precedent narrow-minded catholic regime in Austria induced better and more intelligent men than I was to cherish this hope. Practically all my friends and teachers did so, including my own father who certainly was a kindly and humane man. None of us as much as suspected that the word "selection", when used by these rulers, meant murder. I regret these writings not so much for the undeniable discredit they reflect on my person as for their effect of hampering the future recognition of the dangers of domestication. (From Nobel Prize website)

He told Nisbett that he came to understand the evil of Nazism "surprisingly late" when in 1943 or 1944 he saw transports of people bound for the concentration camps.

In one sense it really does not matter whether Lorenz did, at least for a time, subscribe to Nazi ideology. One may judge him odious, even evil, as many did when that Nobel Prize award was announced and that 1940s paper became widely known. However, the value of his ideas and observations as science are the only judgment that a history of a science should make, and they certainly were valuable. In another sense, though, it does matter. Scientists do have a responsibility to anticipate the possible corruption of their work by evil people in support of evil causes. To work actively to assist in that corruption is to damage, perhaps irreparably, the science itself. It certainly makes life difficult for those who believe in the science but not its corruption.

As noted at the start of this chapter, classical ethology seemed for a time to be eclipsed by the rise of sociobiology in the mid-1970s. Ethology, however, lives on, largely in the form of animal behavioral ecology. The study of animal behavior in the wild has increased considerably. And rising numbers of people, especially those working on physiological mechanisms of drives and emotions, are happy to use the word as a label identifying the science that they do – a kind of generalized evolutionary-physiological approach, a neuro-ethology, aimed at understanding the multiple causes of behavior. In that sense it is Lorenz's old friend, Tinbergen, who in the end wielded the greatest influence.

Sociobiology

There is a view that sociobiology is merely a continuation of ethology using a different theoretical framework. It is certainly the case that ethology, as the increasingly catholic discipline of the study of animal behavior, with its tentative forays into human behavior, was not in any strong sense shown to be wrong and as a result of such error sociobiology then took its place. The simple truth is that ethology never did deliver as a science of comparative behavior, there being relatively few systematic studies using homology apart from Lorenz's work on ducks and Tinbergen's and his students' on gulls. Even in his Nobel acceptance speech Lorenz chose, oddly, to discuss analogy as a source of knowledge, not homology. More importantly, comparative studies had a very old-fashioned ring about them in the 1960s and 1970s. By contrast, sociobiology presented a set of ideas seemingly so compelling and arresting that most just lost interest in the kinds of studies mandated by ethology. In short, ethology looked like old science; sociobiology in 1975 was new, and it was new because it was directly related to what many thought the most significant advance in evolutionary theory since the modern synthesis of 50 years before. As such, it is as good an example that there is of the principle of specific, in sociobiology's case very specific, application.

There is, of course, nothing of significance in a name. Sociobiology was a word coined at a conference in New York in 1948 to depict an interdisciplinary science located somewhere between ecology and physiology on the one side and psychology and sociology on the other. It had little currency until the American biologist E.O. Wilson published a massively influential book bearing the title *Sociobiology: The New Synthesis* in 1975. The name stuck. Social ecology and social ethology were other phrases used. Here, for convenience, sociobiology will refer to the grouping of new ideas and methodologies for the study of animal behavior that arose in the 1960s, that were distinctively different from the core ideas of ethology, and that had three principal foci: altruism (frequently referred to as selfish gene theory as a result of another hugely influential book by the English biologist Richard Dawkins in 1976), game theory, and behavioral ecology. The key new idea was the "genes' eye view" of evolution, specifically behavioral evolution. As in the case of ethology, sociobiology had little immediate impact on psychology but it did lead to bitter controversy at the merest hint that it might be applied to understanding human nature.

At the heart of the whole story is the search for the causes of evolution. Chapter 3 depicted evolutionary biology as a science at relative ease with itself in 1959, a hundred years after the publication of the *Origins*. As indeed it was. All traces of Lamarck were gone; everyone accepted the processes of variation, selection, and transmission as the bases of evolutionary change; and the mechanisms of genetics as the bases of variation and transmission with selection acting upon individual phenotypes. The causal role, if any, of development and behavior remained unresolved, as is still the case today, but the fundamentals of evolutionary theory were widely held to be agreed and understood. Two issues, however, were about to combine to form a problem, the solution of which would be a real change to the theory. One of these was for long so vague as to seem almost a trivial terminological difference between biologists. The other was a specific class of behaviors which were termed altruistic. Both had been present in Darwin's first book but neither attracted much attention.

Darwin would have certainly approved of Karl Popper's falsifiability as the criterion of demarcation of science from pseudoscience. Ever on the lookout for phenomena that might challenge, perhaps even falsify, his theory, what he referred to as "difficulties" and "objections," Darwin had pondered the case of sterile insect castes. Here were animals whose marvelous arrays of specialist adaptations, including behavioral adaptations, had made them exemplars of the need for explanations of design, which Darwin's theory was providing without having to have recourse to a Designer. Yet unable to reproduce themselves, for whom and for what purpose had such adaptations arisen? In trying to answer this "difficulty," Darwin had done something that no-one much noticed or attributed any importance to for close on a hundred years. Throughout the *Origins* and in much of his other writings, the individual organism is what is at the heart of the theory. It is individuals that compete, survive and reproduce. Yet, having posed the problem of the sterile insects, he then disposed of it by saying it really wasn't much of a difficulty at all because "if such insects had been social, and it had been *profitable to the community* that a number should have been annually born capable of work, but incapable of procreation, I can see no difficulty in this having been effected through natural selection" (italics added). In his phrase "profitable to the community" Darwin was saying that the adaptations of the sterile individual animals are for the good of the group. What he had done was switched in his answer to the question of what the most important unit of evolution is – is it the individual or is it the social group, the community, the species? – from the individual, which pervades all of the rest of the book, to the group. He had switched the focus of his theory, or at least raised the question of what that focus should be, probably without realizing it, because that was a question he didn't think needed answering at the time. Perhaps it did not seem to be a question at all because in attempting to account for the big issue, namely how new species arise by way of selection, bringing into the account the social group must have seemed a small matter. In fact it later became a commonplace for explanations to be couched in terms of the "good of the species" and, during the early part of the twentieth century, communities of species, ecological systems and even the entire biosphere were invoked as being what particular characteristics of individuals were "for the good of." Such "naive group selectionism" as it is sometimes referred to, became almost a virtue in the 1940s and 1950s, when systems theory, whose central purpose was understanding the integration of complexly organized entities as is seen in social insects or human organizations like companies or even whole countries, was fashionable.

What had initially troubled Darwin was that sterile insects appear, as it would be put a hundred years later, to behave altruistically. Indeed, by the 1960s, altruistic behavior was coming to be seen as a phylogenetically very wide spread and common form of behavior. Altruism for biologists is any behavior which actually or potentially results in loss of fitness for the animal displaying the behavior, the donor, whilst increasing the fitness of another, the recipient. Such behavior was easily and widely observed and judged altruistic without any actual measurement of costs and benefits being made. Those sterile insect castes provided a prime example. Sterile worker bees defending their hive to the death was the most obvious. The giving of warning signals of approaching danger or the direct nurturing of others were also well documented. And around this time behavioral ecology, an extension of the ethologist's approach to seeing instinctive behaviors as adaptive, using formal mathematical modeling centered on the notion of optimality, was expanding and real numbers could be attached to assumptions about costs and benefits. So not only had altruism in animals moved center-stage, but it had done so within an increasingly quantifiable field.

In an influential book published in 1962 by Vero Wynne-Edwards, a Scottish ecologist, group selection was consistently offered as an explanation for numerous examples of social behavior, especially those labeled altruistic. Because the book was well written and explicit in its arguments in favor of the general importance of group selection, it was widely noticed and came in for critical comment. In particular, the British evolutionist John Maynard Smith and G.C. Williams in the United States were prompted to respond. The argument against Wynne Edwards went like this: if, for example, bird flocks were regulating their reproductive output for the good of the group, and such regulation included reducing reproduction as well as increasing it depending upon environmental circumstances, then in the fullness of time mutant birds would arise whose reproductive output is not so constrained, and the unconstrained reproduction being heritable, the mutant birds would come to dominate the population. Group selection is thus inherently unstable, including when it is being used to explain altruistic behavior. All agreed that *in theory* group selection might account for some altruistic behaviors that appeared inexplicable when seen within the context of individual selection, but because of its inherent instability it is highly unlikely for all cases of such behavior in all the many different species displaying it to be so explained. But then how was it to be explained? Individual selection alone cannot provide understanding, and group selection was argued to be too weak as an explanation of what was turning out to be an embarrassingly widespread behavior. What had seemed a trivial terminological shift from individuals to groups suddenly assumed real theoretical significance. Darwin's first thoughts were correct, even as his answer made the point: this was a real difficulty for his theory.

The answer was given by a young graduate student at the University of London by the name of William Hamilton. According to Ullica Segerstrale, Hamilton had been much neglected as a shy research student working on "the genetics of altruism." It is said that J.B.S. Haldane, one of the original three founders of the modern synthesis who had worked at University College London (the original University of London which later became one of its largest colleges) for decades but left in 1957, had in a quip to colleagues anticipated the essence of Hamilton's theory. Haldane, though, had retired, but at UCL at the time was Maynard Smith, a close colleague of Haldane's who was to be so central to these events. Maynard Smith actually met Hamilton early on, but forgot having done so. It is extraordinary that Hamilton had to struggle on his own. There were two reasons for this. One was that Hamilton was constructing mathematical models of the genetics of altruism which few at first could understand. The second was the very notion of the genetics of altruism. The Nazis and all that they had wrought in Europe were still a very real and terrible memory for many at that time. Any attempt to explain a noble social behavior in genetical terms was just too close to the bone of an obscene ideology. So Hamilton received little encouragement. In the event, he did eventually have his work published in *The Journal of Theoretical Biology* in 1964. Two years later the American evolutionist G.C. Williams published *Adaptation and Natural Selection* which made a powerful case for the same set of ideas, and in a more accessible way than Hamilton's mathematics. Between them Hamilton and Williams changed evolutionary theory. Wilson's *Sociobiology* of 1975 and Dawkins' *The Selfish Gene* of 1976 presented these changes to a much wider audience.

Hamilton and Williams did not deny the importance of individuals, or even groups, in the evolutionary process. But they were pointing at something else as absolutely crucial to how evolution works, and this something else was the gene, or more correctly genes in the plural, which they argued should be seen as being at the heart of evolutionary theory. This was not in their role as the mechanism for variation and transmission that the modern synthesis understood, but genes as the central *unit* of evolution. This was why Hamilton's analysis had focused on those sterile insects of Darwin. Hamilton had two reasons for doing so. One was the phylogenetic distribution of altruistic behaviors which indicated their repeated and independent evolution in the Hymenoptera (bees, wasps, and ants) and Isoptera (termites). The second was because these are orders of insects that are haplo-diploid. We ourselves, and indeed most vertebrates, are diploid in that each of us have pairs of each chromosome in most of our cells. But while insects like bees are diploid if they are females, the males are haploid. Haploid means that the cells bear unpaired, single, chromosomes, and they do so because the males develop from the unfertilized eggs of the female. The result of haplo-diploidy is that males have neither fathers nor sons, and females are more closely related genetically to their sisters than they are to their mothers. Exactly how the sums work out depends upon how many females and males are actually reproducing within each social colony – in bee hives, for example, that number is usually around eight – but whatever that number, the sterile female workers have an unusually close degree of genetic relatedness to their sisters. (It should be noted that, of course, all the members of a species bear a high degree of genetic identity to one another. That is what defines them as conspecifics. But they do also all display small degrees of genetic variation, and it is that small difference that is being considered.)

It is, reasoned Hamilton, the odd genetic make-up of Hymenoptera and Isoptera that is the key to understanding why altruistic behaviors are present to such a high degree in these animals. Sterile female workers "devote" their lives to caring for their sisters because what matters is not individual survival and reproduction but the survival and propagation of genes. So it is not just the fitness of individuals that matters but the fitness of individuals *plus* all those closely genetically related to them. He called this inclusive fitness. From inclusive fitness comes the related notion of kin selection, which replaces individual or group selection. To repeat, what matters are not individuals or groups, but genes. It is genes that are the crucial units of selection. And when, from the point of view of a particular bee or termite, there is a high probability of another bee or termite sharing significant numbers of identical genes then their survival becomes almost as important as that of the particular animal.

There is another way of putting this. There are two ways of propagating genes. One is by the individual organism reproducing itself. The other is for the individual to assist those with whom it shares a high proportion of its genes to reproduce because in that way there is a high probability that many of its own genes will be reproduced in the offspring of its genetic relatives.

The same must apply to all organisms, including diploid animals, though the degree of altruism is somewhat reduced because so too is the probability of sharing identical genes. For example, it has been repeatedly documented in hundreds of species of birds and mammals that individuals frequently spend a part of their lives helping others to reproduce, when the time and energy thus spent could have been dedicated to reproducing their own offspring. The famous example is that of Florida scrub jays, over half of all breeding pairs studied having, on average, two nonreproducing helpers. In only 4 percent of observed cases were the helpers not close genetic kin of the breeding pairs, and in most cases they were themselves older siblings to the young they were defending against predators and nurturing with food. Woolfenden and Fitzpatrick, the original observers of these jays, were able to show that pairs receiving such help successfully reared significantly more young than those without such help; they also demonstrated the complex nature of the interaction between such kin selected behavior and the ecology of these birds, including the advantages to the helpers in terms of themselves becoming successful breeders. It is not that kin selection overrides individual selection; individual fitness matters just as much as those of close genetic kin. That was precisely Hamilton's point.

Similar altruistic behaviors have been well documented in a variety of mammals such as jackals, lions, and a dozen different species of primate. The American social biologist Robert Trivers extended the concept of inclusive fitness to an understanding of parental behaviors and parent–offspring conflict. Contrary to the idealistic and romantic view that parents will love and nurture their young under any and every circumstance, Trivers had observed serious, and potentially dangerous, conflict between monkey mothers and their offspring. He used an extension of Hamilton's theory to explain this by taking a gene's-eye view of what is happening. The keys to understanding parent–offspring conflict is that while monkey young are 50 percent genetically related to their parents, they are *on average* 50 percent related to their siblings (sibs) and only 25 percent related to half-sibs (which in monkeys is most frequently the case). So while it is in any young animal's inclusive fitness interest to maintain parental nurturance focused upon itself (until a point is reached where the costs of doing this become so high that it begins to damage the inclusive fitness even of the young), at some point it is in the inclusive fitness of the parents to invest in other offspring. That is when conflict occurs. The Trivers' model has been supported by studies of vervet monkey living in rich and poor ecologies where the degree of conflict in the same species varies in predictable ways as the environment determines life-time differences in the number of young mothers can have. Stephen Emlen even observed that the African white-fronted bee-eater males often harass and disrupt the attempts to breed of their own sons, with the young males then joining their fathers' nests as helpers. Many other instances of often otherwise inexplicable behavior were recorded and explained using Hamilton's ideas.

Hamilton's Rule, as it came to be known, states that a behavior will evolve if the cost to the donor is outweighed by the gain to the beneficiary multiplied by the degree of genetic kinship. Some geneticists have subsequently argued that the notion of inclusive fitness is subsumed by classical population genetic models of frequency-dependent fitness differences, but nobody doubts that behaviors disadvantageous to one animal will evolve more easily if the beneficiaries are closely related. There are other complications, like the necessity to consider what are called fitness conversion factors (for example, older animals are inherently less fit than younger animals and so altruism should be skewed towards young genetic kin) and the likelihood that altruism will also be biased in favor of close kin, not those that are distant. There is actually nothing simple about selfish gene theory.

It took a few years for the consequences of Hamilton's papers and Williams' book, and then the work of Trivers and others, to be felt in the science of animal behavior. The Wilson and

Dawkins books then accelerated the process. The effects were first seen, of course, in the pages of scholarly journals like *Animal Behavior*, and these then spilled over into the teaching texts. Standard, and often excellent, books used for courses on animal behavior before 1975 were rapidly replaced by new works centered on selfish gene theory by the late 1970s. Other developments, notably in behavioral ecology and game theory, more of which below, added impetus to these changes, but the principal driver of what was nothing less than a revolution in the way people thought about evolution and designed their observations and experiments on behavior, was selfish gene theory. The study of animal behavior was from that time utterly changed from that of classical ethology.

One of the serious criticisms of selfish gene theory is that it is an exercise in extreme reductionist thinking. In his classic 1966 book Williams had written that "the real goal of development is the same as that of all other adaptations, *the continuance of the dependent germ plasm*" (italics added). In the opening page of *Sociobiology* Wilson declared: "the organism is only DNA's way of making more DNA." In 1982, Dawkins wrote that "all adaptations are for the preservation of DNA: DNA itself just is." This certainly sounds like reductionism of some kind. But reductionism comes in a number of different forms and sociobiology conforms to none in any novel way. Ontological reductionism asserts the materialist or physicalist view that all is chemistry and physics, and in subscribing to this sociobiology is no different from any other science. Nor does sociobiology preach methodological reductionism. After all, it is the study of the behavior of whole animals. Theory does not nullify practice. Is it explanatory reductionism? There is an element of this. Explanatory reductionism claims that complex phenomena are best explained in terms of events occurring at the most fundamental level, and since social behaviors are products of evolution then such behaviors must be *part* caused by selected genetic differences between animals. But this is not a belief confined to selfish gene sociobiology. Furthermore, sociobiologists widely acknowledge all other causes of behavior, be they developmental, individual intelligence, and even cultural. The philosophically really serious form of reductionism, theory reduction, is concerned with the formal deduction of one theory from another. No sociobiologist has ever even attempted theory reduction.

How sociobiology is unique is that, if statements like those of Williams and others quoted above mean anything, it is adherence to *metaphysical* genetic reductionism. It is a response to the age-old question of "what is everything for?" or "what is life really about?" The answer from selfish gene theory that it is genes, DNA, that it is all about may strike, does strike, many as odd. But then it is an odd question for scientists to raise in the first place. However, it certainly isn't clear that metaphysics has driven thinking by the sociobiologists. Rather, the metaphysics followed the realization of the importance of the units of selection question to evolutionary theory, and the assumption that DNA, in the role of what came to be called a replicator, is that unit.

Characteristically it was Dawkins and Williams who developed the materialist response to the criticism that selfish gene theory is a form of genetic mysticism. This took the form of replicator theory as an alternative view to how evolution really works. A replicator is something that can make an accurate copy of itself. It does not strive consciously to do so. Replicators are not intentional agents. They merely copy themselves because doing so is inherent in their structure. In the natural world true replicators are very rare entities. The offspring of sexually reproducing organisms are never copies of their parents. Sex gametes are never replicators of parent cells. Even somatic cells produced by ordinary cell division are not good copies of their parent cells. But what are replicators in both meiosis and mitosis are the genes that cells contain. The DNA molecules unzip and then reconstitute themselves, near perfectly because errors do occur. When different replicators overlap in terms of the conditions that are right for their copying of themselves, then they compete. Again there is no intentional agency here. They are just different replicating entities interacting with surrounding conditions, which includes the presence of other replicators. Some replicators utilize these conditions better than others, and thus are introduced selection filters that screen out less effective replicators. In the process of competing for the resources that allow replication to occur some replicators evolved close relationships with other replicators, and even protective coating, a cell, or aggregates of cells, a phenotype, which Dawkins labeled a vehicle. Others, like Waddington and Hull, disliking the connotation of absolute control by the replicators over the passive vehicles preferred terms like operator or interactor because they, correctly, understood that vehicles can evolve causal powers, like intelligence, that are not directly linked to replicators. But no matter. It is the vehicle upon which selection acts, and in passing through selection filters they do so in order that replicators may replicate themselves.

It is in this sense that replicators design effective vehicles, but design does not mean intentional design. It is simply a hugely concatenated sequence of events by which replicators interacting with each other and with the selection filters of the environment result in variable phenotypes. Dawkins' use of the metaphor "the selfish gene" was a form of shorthand that he has been at pains to unpack into nonintentional language, just as he and others unpacked the "gene for this" and "gene for that" into inherited genetic differences between individuals that part cause pheno- typic traits. But many people are careless readers or listeners and they take away wrong meanings. That is not because the science is necessarily wrong, but because its presentation may be flawed. That is one of the lessons that the sociobiology controversy should have taught anyone seeking to introduce evolutionary thinking into the social sciences.

Sociobiology was born of a change in evolutionary thinking and its application to explanations of animal behavior. The writings of Hamilton and Williams in 1964 and 1966 contain virtually no references to humans; they were technical exercises in evolutionary theory. If that was where it had remained the result might have been good-natured debate amongst scholars as to whether replicators could have such extraordinary power. But some did extend it to humans, and that was where the trouble really began. Indeed whilst not the first to do so, it was specific- ally E.O. Wilson's *Sociobiology* book that triggered the hostility to this way of looking at evolution, and its supposed consequences for understanding human nature. What Wilson did was sand- wich what was essentially an otherwise well-received text on animal social behavior between opening and closing chapters, the first of which antagonized many by announcing the immi- nent take over of all of biology by either sociobiology or molecu- lar biology, and the last, which antagonized even more, by considering the application of sociobiology to humans. Reread- ing those (in)famous chapters 28 years on, the first chapter seems much the more provocative, and we now know was nonsense.

Wilson had predicted the imminent death of the likes of neuroscience and psychology and in this was simply wrong. The last chapter, which really set the stage for what was perhaps the most bitter and ill-tempered dispute in twentieth-century science, now seems really rather tame. True, statements like "Scientists and humanists should consider together the possibility that the time has come for ethics to be removed temporarily from the hands of the philosophers and biologicized," and suggestions that human warfare may result in increases in inclusive fitness for the survivors, do seem to be rather raw applications of biology to human affairs. But that last chapter, which was in fact relatively short and very sparse on detail or evidence, contained much speculative handwaving about language and culture, group selection is clearly advocated as an important aspect of human biology, and social scientists sympathetic to biology, like Robin Fox and Lionel Tiger, are cited. This was no hard-nosed application of the "humans are just like ants" variety of the social Darwinism of Wilfred Trotter who during World War One had argued ridiculously that differences between nations were the result of differences in the animal instincts that dominated them, or the open racism of the race theorists of that time.

Nonetheless, the reaction to Wilson's book was immediate and heated. A *Sociobiology Study Group of Science for the People* was established almost immediately after publication, and included some notable left-wing academics from the Boston area, especially Richard Lewontin and Stephen J. Gould of Harvard University. Wilson too was at Harvard. Meetings were held, letters written to newspapers, especially those in which *Sociobiology* had been favorably reviewed, protests were mounted, and books criticizing Wilson were written. Details can be found in Segerstrale's history of the events that she lived through and experienced for herself. The sheer scale of the protests seem now to be quite out of proportion to a book on animal behavior that also contained some fatuous predictions about the future of the biological sciences and a brief speculative foray into human behavior. In February of 1978 a meeting of the American Association for the Advancement of Science held in Washington DC included a two day meeting on Sociobiology. As Wilson was preparing to deliver his paper, about ten people charged onto the stage and, according to Segerstrale, were chanting "Racist Wilson you can't hide, we charge you with genocide." Wilson then had a jug of iced water emptied over his head. Stephen Chorover, a psychologist at the MIT, published in 1979 a book entitled *From Genesis to Genocide* in which he compared Wilson's sociobiology with Nazi biological doctrine. But it is simply not possible to find anywhere in Wilson's work any form of analysis, or casual aside, which preaches either genocide or racism. Indeed in his 1976 book Wilson clearly disassociated himself even from Lorenz's ethology. He was also at pains to distance himself from Galtonesque claims about the inheritance of intelligence, an issue that had resurfaced in psychology in the late 1960s. So what was his crime? He had advocated a view, according to his critics, that was a form of genetic determinism. His stance was that people are what they are because of their genes, and this is irremediably so. He had left culture out of the picture, or when he did write of it he equated it with the social behavior of other species. None of this is correct. As Segerstrale points out, to get from the actual text to these accusations people were interpreting meaning. Dawkins' *The Selfish Gene* added fuel to the fire, even though in his final chapter Dawkins coined the word "memes" to account for human behavior. Memes, he argued, are the cultural analogues of genes, and another form of those rare entities, replicators (see next chapter for a fuller account of memetics). Indeed the last two sentences of the book read: "We are built as gene machines and cultured as meme machines, but we have the power to turn against our creators. We, alone on earth, can rebel against the tyranny of the selfish replicators." Perhaps not many of the critics of sociobiology read or understood those words, because Dawkins too was denounced as a genetic determinist.

Psychology, by and large, did not enter much into the argument at that time. It certainly did not incorporate any of the main elements of the Hamilton/Williams theory into the body of its ideas. A survey of both the *Psychological Review* and *Psychological Bulletin*, the two principle theoretical journals of psychology, over the period 1975 to 1990, reveals a lofty indifference to the sociobiological thesis. Unsurprisingly this was not the case for interdisciplinary journals like *The Behavioral and Brain Sciences* which frequently entered into the fray through the 1980s. What is, perhaps, surprising was the support given to the sociobiological thesis by an emerging school of anthropologists making common cause with sociobiology. *Evolutionary Biology and Human Social Behavior: An Anthropological Perspective* of 1979 provided what Wilson's book had not, which was a serious and concerted attempt by the likes of Richard Alexander, William Irons, and others to interpret at least some aspects of human cultures, such as kinship categories and inheritance patterns, within an evolutionary framework that included selfish gene theory. Napoleon Chagnon's studies of the Yanomamo people of Venezuela, perhaps because his work centered upon warfare and the sexual prizes of aggressive and violent behavior, and hence of inclusive fitness benefits of such behavior, attracted particular attention. (It might be noted that the eruption of serious feuding within the community of anthropologists in 2000 following the publication of the book *Darkness in El Dorado* by the journalist Patrick Tierney, which detailed the supposed wrong doings by doctors and anthropologists, including Chagnon, against the Yanomamo people, is a measure of how little the scars have healed. A commission of inquiry by the American Anthropological Association found all of Tierney's most serious charges to be without foundation.)

Incorrect interpretation and misguided allegations aside, some serious criticisms of sociobiology were made by formidable opponents like Lewontin and Gould who pursued the case against sociobiology relentlessly. Among the numerous significant criticisms, including carelessness in demarcating the "'natural' suture lines for evolutionary dynamics" in Lewontin's nice phrase, reification, conflation and confusion of levels (some of these very like the points made by Lehrman and others against Lorenz 30 years before) was the charge of adaptationism. Adaptations entered into the sociobiological thesis as the means by which genes propagate themselves. Replicators construct adaptations as the means by which they can successfully replicate themselves, and so adaptations are central to the sociobiological case. But, argued Gould and Lewontin, sociobiology was insufficiently aware of the plurality of causes in complex biological systems, and was largely an exercise in the telling of adaptationist just-so stories in which all phenotypic traits, including complex culturally determined behaviors and practices, are incorrectly designated as adaptations for the good of those unlikely entities, the genes. This is a not insubstantial point and 20 years later was to be repeatedly leveled at evolutionary psychology, so it will be dealt with at greater length in the next chapter.

It remains to deal briefly with those other elements of socio-biology, behavioral ecology and game theory, which were rather less contentious forays of evolutionary biology into the social sciences. Behavioral ecology is the direct descendent from Tinbergens functional "why" question. What is different from the ethological approach to understanding that behavior has evolved because it contributes to individual fitness is that it buys in to the enlarged conception of fitness as gene-centered, and hence to the importance of kinship and inclusive fitness, and it measures functional value using quantitative modeling. Like everything else in this chapter, behavioral ecology is a part of the science of animal behavior, the extension of which to humans came after its initial development by biologists studying the behavior of animals under natural conditions. A significant amount of work in this area has concerned the foraging and processing of food. For example, crows that feed on whelks have first to break open the shells. They do this by dropping the whelks onto rocks, and this is a situation ripe for quantification. The costs, measured in terms of the energy needed to fly to a specific height and the number of times that a whelk must be dropped before it is smashed open, can be traded against the benefits, the calorific value of each whelk. Observation of actual behavior, of the height from which the whelks are dropped and the average frequency for which this must be done when they are dropped from different heights, can be compared with the predictions of a simple model that computes what the optimal behavior which yields the greatest benefits against the least costs is. When this is done the observed minimum flight per whelk is satisfyingly close to the predictions of the model. Many other examples of elegant studies that compare the predictions of quantitative models with actual behavior, be it instances of load carrying in other species of animal or the size of social groups and the way this varies in response to degree of predation or the availability of food resources can be found in Krebs and Davies classic text on behavioral ecology.

By the early 1980s anthropologists of a Darwinian bent were studying human behavior from this perspective. The practices and traditions studied included the spacing of the births of children, degrees of polygamy, the sizes of hunting groups, and the numbers of domesticated animals maintained, to name but a few. The original, relatively simple optimality models used with animals had to be refined into more dynamic instruments that take into account fluctuating states of both the individuals whose behavior is being observed and the circumstances under which they live. The most important question raised by such studies concerns the root causes of the behaviors observed. It seems highly unlikely that altering herd size as family and larger social group circumstances change such that the amount of food available matches the needs of people, for example, is the product of evolved traits that are triggered like fixed action patterns in stickleback fish. Humans have the capacity to reason, take decisions, and learn from the experience of others. This has always been known. That they act to further their own interests and those close to them has always been known. That they manipulate the world in ways that work best has always been known. One of the oldest schools of cultural anthropology is that of the adaptationists who believed the best way to understand culture is that it ensures survival across a range of ecologies by providing adaptations, cultural adaptations, that human biology without culture cannot do. So isn't human behavioral ecology just plain old-fashioned cultural anthropology of the adaptationist variety but dressed up in numbers and with selfish gene theory tucked under its explanatory arm? Many social scientists, including psychologists, believed the answer to the question was yes; that human behavioral ecology was and still is old wine in new bottles. This was certainly the view of a number of influential psychologists who represented a specific approach on how to apply evolutionary theory to the study of the human mind. They will be considered in the next chapter.

Game theory, by contrast with the other methods and approaches outlined in this chapter, is an import into biology from economics, and remains a central conceptual tool of contemporary microeconomics. First developed in the 1940s by the mathematician John van Neumann and the economist Oskar Morgenstern, game theory is a means of mathematically modeling the interaction of rational, decision-making agents whose concern is to maximize their own utilities (that is, they try to do the best for themselves) as they interact with other agents within the framework of a specific game. The agents do not necessarily have to be individuals. They could be companies, armies, or even whole countries where decision-making powers are vested in boards of directors, staff headquarters, or governments. Social scientists will as often consider agents to be aggregates of individuals, like competing banks or supermarkets, as they are to consider them as individuals. When game theory was introduced into the study of animal behavior by Maynard Smith and others, the assumption, of course, was that the agents are individual animals employing strategies that maximize their fitness.

Now game theory is of interest to psychologists because it has yielded experimental situations that have a potential for telling us very interesting things about the human mind. Take the example of the ultimatum game. In this game an individual, the proposer, makes a take-it-or-leave-it offer on how to split a sum of money with another person. If the proposer is turned down by the person to whom the offer is being made, neither agent receives any money at all. On first consideration, one might expect that almost any offer by the proposer would be accepted, because any amount is better than nothing. The person to whom the proposal is made is getting something for nothing. But what has been found in studies carried out in Germany, the United States, Israel, the former Yugoslavia and Japan is that low offers, anything less than around 20 percent of the amount to be split, is almost always rejected. Usually only amounts twice that are generally accepted. Whilst on the surface these countries might be considered to represent very different cultures, a closer examination of just who the participants in the experiments were, or even whether, say, Israel and Japan do in general consist of very different cultures when money is at issue, leaves doubts as to whether the findings are truly cross-cultural. More research, as they say, is needed. But the results are fascinating, and one interpretation is that all humans have an innate norm of fairness. Perhaps, some hint, Wilson's 1976 claim for the biologizing of ethics deserves closer examination.

Game theory offers an undoubtedly powerful methodology to psychology as well as to economists. But given the origins of game theory it can hardly be claimed to be the application of evolutionary biology in the social sciences, even though it has been incorporated into evolutionary analysis, and such analysis used iterative game playing which has been a real contribution by evolutionary game theorists. But if the science of mind has found this a useful tool, it is economics that it must largely thank, not evolutionary biology.

All in all, then, what lessons do ethology and sociobiology have to offer the revived evolutionary psychology of the 1990s? Some, conceptually, from ethology such as the revival of thinking in broad terms of instincts and the role of the environment of evolutionary adaptedness; but selfish gene theory, and its corollary, the adapted nature of behavior and the processes and mechanisms that drive that behavior such that genes are preserved and propagated, certainly had to bear real conceptual force for anyone applying evolutionary thought to the behavior and minds of humans. Another lesson, one spelled out repeatedly in this and previous chapters, is that principle of specific application. There was another lesson to be learned. It is that one has to be very, very, careful when writing about evolution and the human mind in edgy political times. The Nazis might have been a fading memory in the 1970s. But the civil rights struggle in the United States, the Vietnam war, and the increasing prominence of the effects of the apartheid regime in South Africa made that decade a politically peevish period. It is, of course, every person's right to dress their science up in an ideology if they so choose. But for those who find the mixing of science and ideology distasteful, if not plain wrong, then they had better steel themselves to possible distortions and misuse of their science because there is a good chance that someone is going to do just that.

CHAPTER SEVEN

Contemporary Evolutionary Psychology

James Mark Baldwin was the first evolutionary psychologist but he had no disciples, no followers or converts who spread the word and formed a school of thought. Eighty years were to pass before that was to happen, and then it owed nothing at all to Baldwin's work which remains known only to a handful of developmentalists and evolutionary epistemologists. As stated in the preface, it is not possible to provide a historical perspective on the evolutionary psychology of the present day. Lineages of ideas cannot be detected with any clarity, and the significance of individuals, concepts, or approaches cannot yet be assessed. No reliable judgments can be made from such close temporal quarter as to what is the trivial, if often sensational, and what will be important and enduring. It is all too close to the here and now. The period from the mid-1960s to the mid-1980s can and will be briefly considered as the most immediate causes of the revival of evolutionary thinking in psychology. But the phrase "evolutionary psychology" dates back only about 16 years, and so lacking a historical framework, the area in general will be selectively outlined, as will be the problems and challenges that it faces. It is also necessary to consider the background conditions that shaped the appearance of modern evolutionary psychology, and the reactions to it. In large part these concern evolutionary theory itself. (No claim is made for this chapter as a comprehensive review of contemporary evolutionary psychology. It is not. For that there are a number of recently published and easily available texts.)

Evolutionary Theory from 1959

If the theory of evolution looked like a science at ease with itself during the centenary celebrations of the publication of Darwin's 1859 book, this was not the case in 1982 when the anniversary of his death was marked by conferences and various publications. Two things had happened during those 23 years. One was the appearance of rival theories of how evolution occurs, and the other was the repoliticization of evolution and its application to humans. Both were of relevance to the reappearance of evolutionary thinking in psychology.

The difference between 1950's biology and that of the 1980s was primarily the enormous increase in knowledge, especially of the molecular basis of life. It is impossible to overestimate the importance of the certain understanding of the structure of DNA specifically and the workings within cells more generally – to the point where, in the light of a rampant molecular biology which laid out the facts, some questioned the point of theory of any kind. Others attempted a radical restatement of evolution within a more physico-chemical setting. Thus were born nonequilibrium thermodynamic and structuralist theories of evolution. These did not stand in contradiction to neo-Darwinism. What they attempted was a recasting of the causal language for the transformation of species in time. Conceptions of how to balance the relative stability of living systems against the diversity and change that characterizes evolution introduced notions of order and entropy in place of variation, selection, and transmission. Most biologists were skeptical and this particular fashion did not last long. However, molecular biology made its mark in other ways. This was bound to occur as increasing knowledge pointed to the immense complexity of subcellular structure and organization. Genes turned out not to be discrete and punctate "beads on a string" of the pre-1950s age of genetics. Instead it began to be understood that they have a massive and rather messy molecular structure smeared across large stretches of chromosomes with a lot of noncoding DNA interspersed amongst the lesser regions that do code for protein. It also began to be understood that genes form complex systems of functionally related but spatially widespread units which interact with one another. Such epistatic (gene-gene) interactions are not the only interactions that genes enter into: they interact dynamically with other cellular molecules, including their own products. Here was a previously untapped source of possible causation of evolutionary change.

In the 1960s several theorists independently advocated neutral theories, which, in essence, asserted that many changes at the intra-cellular level are not due to selection acting upon mutations, but are due instead to changes in molecular structure, however these may be caused, which are, at least initially, neutral in outcome and hence unexpressed in the phenotype, perhaps for many generations. If unexpressed, such genetic change cannot be affected by natural selection and so might accumulate away from the influence of Darwin's major causal force. In the 1970s, A.C. Wilson offered strong evidence that protein structure change occurs at a constant rate in time, irrespective of rates of reproduction in unit time: if molecular change occurs at approximately the same rates for all species (apart from those with complex behavioral repertoires, which harks back to Baldwin) whatever their reproductive rates, this is, at the very least, at odds with the idea that selection is the only or principal force for evolutionary change. Then in the 1980s, molecular-drive theories were advanced. Whilst previous molecular-based theory argued for additional, and perhaps unselected, sources of variation, molecular-drive theorists offered molecular-level events as autogenous drivers not only of variation but also as sources of selection different and apart from natural selection. Complexity and self-organization theory, which is concerned with explaining, at a wholly theoretical level, how complex and self-organized systems that are "poised between order and chaos" provide the conditions for "evolvability," is a kind of hybrid of nonequilibrium thermodynamic theory and the later molecular-drive theories.

What most such theories did was provide richer sources of variation and selection within a more complexly structured conception of evolution. Some, especially complexity theory, opened up, again, the issue of how individual development enters the picture. They did not, though, challenge the central claims of neo-Darwinism that selection is a major force for evolutionary change and the only explanation for adaptations. What did make that challenge was punctuated equilibrium theory offered in the 1970s by two paleontologists, Niles Eldredge and Stephen J. Gould. Going against received wisdom that considered the fossil record to be a partial and incomplete record of the history of life forms, and hence which so often fails to show the gradual transitions from one species to another, they argued instead that the fossil record provides a true picture of the history of life on Earth. Contrary to Darwin's own insistent gradualism, and that subsequently of neo-Darwinism, Eldredge and Gould asserted that evolutionary history is characterized by long durations of stability of form interspersed by geologically brief periods of change. Well, perhaps. After an initial, if prolonged, period of opposition, if not outright ridicule, this aspect of punctuated equilibrium theory is now considered a real possibility. Indeed, it was realized, some of Darwin's own writings point to some similar patterns of stasis and relatively rapid speciation. In part it is a semantic issue. What does rapid mean in geological time? How gradual is gradual? Furthermore, Eldredge and Gould did not dispute the neo-Darwinian maxim that adaptations are the result of microevolution brought about by variation and selection. But what was really radical in their theory was the decoupling of microevolution from macroevolution (speciation).

Other ideas, judged, often wrongly, to be at variance with neo-Darwinism were being forcefully presented around this time. At a meeting of the Royal Society in London in 1978 Gould and Lewontin presented a paper critical of an evolutionary biology that provided an unthinking reliance on the notion of adaptation as the preeminent explanation for the forms and functions of living things. They certainly did not deny the existence and importance of adaptation. What they challenged was what they considered to be the conceptual monopoly that adaptationist thinking held in the minds of too many evolutionists. It was a call for a greater pluralism in evolutionary biological thought. Subsequently, Lewontin developed a critical stance on the conception of adaptations as responses to problems posed by environmental challenges on passive organisms. He advocated instead a more interactive conception of organisms in part creating their environments and not simply reacting to them. This has since come to be called niche-construction in a significant theoretical development by John Odling-Smee and his colleagues. For his part, Gould developed the notion of exaptation. Darwin had recognized what he called "pre-adaptations," which are phenotypic traits whose functions are not the same as those for which they were originally selected. Gould added to this by claiming that many adaptive traits may also have originated for nonadaptive reasons and have since been coopted to adaptive function. Traits that originally had different functions, or no functions at all, he lumped together as exaptations. As will be seen, some critics of evolutionary psychology consider this an important conception.

There is another aspect to any history of evolutionary theory in the second half of the twentieth century. In a recent book, *The Blank Slate*, Steven Pinker, a strong advocate of evolutionary psychology, cites startling results of reputable polls carried out in the late 1990s and early 2000s in the United States. These show that presently around 75 percent of Americans believe in the biblical account of creation as opposed to 15 percent who consider that evolution is the correct view of the origins and history of life. It is safe to assume that the disparity in these figures would be greater the further back in time one goes. One result has been repeated challenges by creationists to the teaching of evolution in American schools. Conservative Christians are not, of course, the only religious fundamentalists opposed to evolution and its teaching, but it is in the United States that these battles have, and still are, being fought. One such major battle in the courts occurred in the early 1980s. And one of the things creationists had latched on to has been the increasing disputation amongst evolutionists since the 1960s. Deeply ignorant of how science works, creationists have argued that disagreement amongst scientists weakens the case for evolution being a correct view of the world. This has given an edge to the disputes within evolutionary biology. In London something approaching open warfare broke out amongst systematists in the 1970s as to the relevance of evolutionary theory to the classification of organisms and serious attempts to resuscitate Lamarckian theory in the 1980s did not help. The philosopher of science Karl Popper in his autobiography declared that evolutionary theory is "not a testable scientific theory, but a metaphysical research program – a possible framework for testable scientific theories." He later retracted but the damage had been done. All this was grist to the creationists' mill.

No biologist now denies the transformation of species in time. In the last two or three decades there have been a number of reports of observed microevolutionary changes in a range of animal and plant species, including Darwin's Galapagos finches. The old criticism of evolution, that it occurs so slowly that it cannot be observed directly but only inferred, no longer holds. Microevolution can occur in a short period of time – just months or a few years – and in a remarkably small number of generations. It has now been directly seen to occur. But what of macroevolution? In the early 1940s Ernst Mayr had argued that a demonstration of the existence of ring species would be the "perfect demonstration of speciation." A ring species is a group of organisms that, through successive migrations in opposite directions around an obstacle, diverges slowly away from the original parent population such that when the migrating populations eventually meet at a point on the opposite side of the obstacle they are sufficiently changed that they can no longer interbreed. One species has become two. No unblemished reports of ring species existed until a study was published in *Nature* in 2001 on speciation in a ring by a team from the University of California. Using both genetic and behavioral evidence from Warblers in Siberia, to the north of the Tibetan plain, they were able to show conclusively that the two species of birds observed there are descendants of the original parent species to the south. Macroevolution too has now been observed under natural conditions.

It is also correct to say that no biologist of any repute now denies that evolution is the proper explanation for the diversity of living forms, their distribution in space, and their ordering into lineages of descent. No biologist denies that selection is a crucial causal force in the evolution of adaptations. The differences concerns exactly how evolution occurs. The putting forward of alternative theories as explanations for the phenomena of this world is a part of the normal process of science. Nonetheless, the use by creationists of these legitimate arguments amongst knowledgeable scientists has left the community of evolutionary scientists somewhat tense and ill humored. Selfish gene theory, itself an advance on neo-Darwinism that has been opposed in some scientific quarters, and especially its application to human behavior, has not improved the temper of the science. Given the general sense that the human mind is a particularly sensitive area for science to tread in, as outlined in chapter 1, an evolutionary science of mind that began to appear in the 1980s was bound to have a mixed reception.

Necessary Precursors in the Main Discipline

Evolutionary thinking in psychology could not have reoccurred without changes at the heart of the main discipline. These had several sources. Much the most important was the collapse of behaviorism in American psychology. Behaviorism had never been the dominating influence in European psychology that it had been in the United States. The major figures in Europe like F.C. Bartlett in England, Jean Piaget in Switzerland, Edouard Claparéde in France, the Gestalt school of psychologists (notably Max Wertheimer, Wolfgang Kohler, and Kurt Koffka) in Germany, and Lev Vygotsky in Russia (Pavlov never saw himself as a psychologist, and had he done so he would not have espoused behaviorism even though behaviorists used his methodology) had never subscribed to the intellectual bankruptcy of American behaviorism whose essence was the banning of hypothesizing on the causes of behavior that could not be directly perceived by the experimenter.

Watson, it will be remembered from chapter 4, had advanced an extreme form of peripheralism with the dogmatic assertion that "there are no centrally initiated processes" and was an advocate of the *tabula rasa* view of the human mind at birth. Subsequent prominent behaviorists like Hull and Skinner did loosen that restriction on central processes somewhat, but the concepts such as schemas (inferred central foci of cognitive organization) or perceptual fields (the innate tendency for perception to be structured in terms of figure and ground) so important to European psychology simply did not exist within the conceptual heartland of behaviorism.

George Mandler points to the significance of World War Two and its technological spin-offs in the information processing industries in changing this. Cybernetics and computers were its immediate postwar products. And during the war many psychologists who were to spearhead the cognitive revolution, like George Miller, were working on war-related problems of perception and signal detection. In England, research into attention by Broadbent, fueled in part by the requirement for practical work in various industries, showed the need for proper theory if psychology was to have successful application. No less important was the rise in the United States of the linguistician, Noam

Chomsky, whose theory of transformational grammar was a radical departure from long accepted ideas on language.

Until the appearance of Chomsky, most psychologists subscribed to the view that language was acquired by children using the same general learning processes that they used to acquire other forms of knowledge ranging from motor skills to spatial maps. Piaget and Skinner were the most prominent proponents of this view, even if the theories they offered were utterly different from each other. The position of Chomsky was then, and has remained since, quite different from either. Chomsky considered all human languages to derive from a universal grammar that is "triggered" by specific linguistic environments to result in children coming to acquire a specific native language from the 6,000 plus languages that exist on earth. Chomsky's is a strong nativist position. Language, he claimed, is an innate organ of mind and the acquisition of specific languages employs learning mechanisms different from those used to acquire other forms of knowledge. The evidence that has gathered over the years since then, be it from signing in deaf children to the development of Creoles, has been in overwhelming support of the Chomsky position, but that is not really the point. What is here was a powerful voice in the 1950s, and it was powerful enough to rout both Skinner in the late 1950s and Piaget some 20 years later, making claims about central processes and mechanisms that *had* to be inferred and could not possibly be directly observed.

That is what was so important about the cognitive revolution in psychology. It allowed psychologists to develop a rich theory of the causes of behavior in terms of central processes and mechanisms. For 50 years psychology had been trapped in an absurd position, equivalent to that of geneticists forbidden from postulating the existence of genes or chemists not being allowed to postulate the reality of entities like atoms or subatomic particles because genes and subatomic particles cannot be perceived with the naked sensors of observers. Now, at last, people could theorize about the existence of different forms of memory, attentional mechanisms, or integrating executive processes, for example, which could lead to predictions and be cashed out into experiments, the results of which were fed back as adjustments to the theory. In a very real sense, it was only with the cognitive revolution that psychology became a science again. And being allowed claims of causes not immediately visible to the eye meant that notions like neural networks of specific form, genetic part-causation and natural selection could be invoked as causes of behavior.

Two other developments in psychology were essential to the rise of evolutionary approaches. One of these was the discovery of constraints on learning. As was seen in the previous chapter, Lorenz had postulated the existence of evolved innate teaching mechanisms without having any evidence whatever as to the existence of constraints on learning that such mechanisms would cause. But within a year a psychologist in the United States was attempting to publish the first evidence for constrained learning in laboratory rats, showing a greater ease of associating taste and smell stimuli with the unconditional stimuli of nausea than with electrical shock. That J. Garcia had a considerable struggle to get his work published initially shows how strong were the prejudices of general process learning theorists, and how powerfully placed they were within scientific psychology. Notions of "preparedness" and "unpreparedness" to learn certain things rather than others began to proliferate, as did phrases like "species-specific defence reactions," surprisingly Lorenzian in flavor for psychologists studying learning in animals in laboratory experiments. And there was much talk of the ecology of learning. All this was the result of an accumulation from the early 1970s onwards of reports of constrained learning in a variety of different species. These included the acquisition of song in song-birds which is powerfully constrained towards the learning of species-specific song; humming-birds able to acquire certain strategies that fit well with their natural foraging behavior; and sex-differences in spatial learning ability in different species of vole which matches their reproductive strategies. By 1984 the Dahlem Workshop on the *Biology of Learning* filled a volume with these and other studies. The similarities to language learning in humans did not go unnoticed. A question began to be asked that echoed one from half a century before, but with an inverted meaning: if domain-specific learning, bearing the hallmarks of the operation of evolved adaptive mechanisms for cognition of events that are significant to the life-history strategies of species occurs widely in nonhumans, might this not also apply to humans? It should be noted that such findings did not negate the possibility that general learning processes exist.

Indeed studies of learning in bees demonstrated characteristics of learning similar to, perhaps identical to, those shown in experiments on laboratory rats. So, it was argued, the constraints might take a variety of forms such as attentional biases or response limitations. But whatever these might be, something is constraining the learning to specific features of the environment, and such constraints must have evolved to make learning efficient. For those of an evolutionary bent what mattered was species-specific constraint on learning; the mechanism, whilst important, was beside the evolutionary point.

Answers, or at least partial answers, to the question posed about the possibility of human learning being similarly constrained began to appear in the early 1980s. They were a result of a change in methodology for studying cognition in very young infants. Sometimes referred to as the looking-time method, it comprised the seating of an infant on the lap of, or close to, one of the child's principal carers, often enough the mother, in front of a television monitor on which various displays appeared. How long the infant stared at a display was timed. This dishabituation method was based on the assumption that infants would pay attention to novel displays longer than they would to material with which they were familiar. The results, in general, pointed to infants having a surprising amount of knowledge relatively soon after birth. In the some of the earliest of these experiments Alan Leslie in England used launching displays, with a stationary ball on the screen being struck by another ball that swings in from the edge of the picture, the previously stationary ball then being launched off the screen and the ball that struck it coming to a halt. This elicits little interest in a six-month-old child, which is without language and does not have the reasoning capacity to analyze and form predictions based on explicit understanding of cause-effect relations. But if the second ball stops before it reaches the stationary ball, and the latter then is launched off the screen, which action-at-a-distance is a violation of the causal texture of the world, then the observing infant displays a high level of interest. These infants displayed an unreasoned appreciation of launching causality and were surprised to see it reversed, and could do so, Leslie argued, "without having to know what a cause 'really' is." This cognitive capacity is not, he considered, a product of gradual development or of prolonged learning experience but the result of the operation of a low-level perceptual mechanism that feeds its computational descriptions of the world to more central cognitive domains like one which is primed to understand the behavior of inanimate objects in the physical world – what some refer to as intuitive physics.

Reneé Baillargeon and her colleagues have further mined this rich seam of research. Female infants as young as 18 weeks (males are a little slower) are surprised at displays that are physically impossible, like the removal of the lower block of two leaving the block perched on top of it hanging in the air, but are unsurprised when the upper block falls to the surface. In a variation on this theme, infants as young as 12 weeks were surprised by blocks which when pushed off the side of a supporting surface remained suspended in mid-air, but showed no interest in displays when the pushed block fell over the side of the support. Using the same method, Karen Wynn and her colleagues at the University of Arizona have shown five-month-old infants to have a basic numerical competence. They expect one object when added to another to result in two objects and not one or three, and that one object removed from an initial display of two should result in one object, not two or none at all. These are well controlled experiments and indicate a knowledge of expected numerical result and not merely that one grouping of objects is more or less than another.

The findings of such studies are not in doubt. How they are to be understood is a matter of some controversy and argument. Broadly speaking there are two kinds of interpretation. One is strongly nativist and very similar to Chomsky's position on language. What such cognitive capacity reveals, especially in infants of just a few months of age much of whose immediate postnatal life is spent in sleep, is that humans come into the world with cognitive mechanisms primed to acquire specific forms of information. The priming may not be precise, but in a world that is unlabelled and which can be partitioned and ordered in a huge number of possible ways, the innate constraints provide a modicum of organizational principles that allow input to sensory systems to be grouped in ways that are consistent with the structure of that world. The slate, in other words, is written upon at birth. The philosopher of mind, Jerry Fodor, refers to this as the new rationalism. The empiricists were wrong, though Plato was certainly not completely right.

The other line of interpretation might be described as a form of developmental empiricism. Using a form of neural modeling known as connectionism, it offers the conception of a limited innate process for computing sensory input, but the cognitive functions that they mediate are not primed for specific contents such as language or physical causal structure. That they eventually come to focus on such limited domains of the world are the result of a complex cascade of developmental events, including the learning afforded during limited wakefulness, such that initially untuned neural networks become tuned to process specific kinds of input.

It is not clear which position will eventually be shown to be correct. What is known is that around half of the human genome is connected in some way with the construction of the human nervous system. It is only a matter of time before advances in neurogenetics tells us exactly how the structure and function of the central nervous system relates to genes. It is also inevitable that the relationships between specific neural structures and psychological processes and mechanisms will be revealed over the coming decades. The coming together of these two bodies of evidence together with increased understanding of the psychological mechanisms of cognition will represent one of the great advances of twenty-first-century science; it will also tell us whether it is the new rationalists or the developmental empiricists who are right.

So, unsolved as this question might yet be, what is clear is that anyone choosing the new rationalist position has a theoretical platform for launching a kind of evolutionary psychology. If the slate is written on at birth, and if what is written comprises domain-specific adaptations for the acquisition of knowledge about what it is important for everyone to know, or a disposition to behave in certain ways in particular circumstances, then suites of genes, perhaps the products of evolutionary selection, must be one of the causes of that writing.

Evolutionary Psychology Reborn

Liberated from the theoretical muteness of behaviorism, encouraged by an increasing evolutionary presence in anthropology, assisted by advances in animal and developmental cognition, and with conceptual predecessors, if weak ones, in ethology but much stronger ties to the more recent sociobiology, a revival of some kind of evolutionary psychology was bound to occur. This began in the mid-to late 1980s and had a number of sources. One influential study, on murder, came in 1988 from Martin Daly and Margo Wilson of McMaster University, specifically the department of psychology – this shift towards work coming out of psychology departments was significant. From an examination of the figures on murder, who is killing who, especially within families, and its consequences, Daly and Wilson concluded that the patterns thus revealed fitted exactly with predictions based on the assumption that:

> species-typical appetites, aversions, motives, emotions, and cognitive structures of all creatures, including *Homo sapiens*, have been shaped by selection to produce social action that is effectively "nepotistic": action that promotes the proliferation of the actor's genetic elements in future generations, by contributing to the survival and reproductive success of the actor's genetic relatives. (Daly and Wilson, 1988b, p. 519)

This is straightforward selfish gene theory applied within the context of a specific if extreme form of human violence. There could be no better example of our principle of specific application.

The figures were unequivocal. When murder is committed within a family setting in the United States, the victim and perpetrator are about 10 times more likely to be nongenetic kin, partners, than genetically related individuals. This is especially dramatically demonstrated in the case of children killed by a stepparent. Figures from North America, Australia, and Britain all showed that a child was around 100 times more likely to be killed by a stepparent than a biological parent. These figures are comparable to those revealed by the ethnographic record of many quite different cultures. The wicked stepparent figure looks to be a cultural universal. Daly and Wilson also showed that in patriarchal societies men take a proprietorial view of their women. Isolation and actual physical encumbrance and mutilation to lessen the possibility of infidelity aside, assumed or actual infidelity is the overwhelming cause of murder of women by men. (Whilst not a part of their study, anthropological evidence reviewed by others from matriarchal cultures where women have relatively free sexual choice, shows the lines of inheritance under such circumstances of greatly increased uncertainty of paternity to be accordingly quite different too.)

Daly and Wilson supported their general thesis by looking at the age distributions of children killed by mothers and fathers and compared them with the ages of children killed by unrelated individuals. They also examined the ages of mothers at the time of the birth of a child who later is killed by that child. In every case, the patterns conform to a selfish gene interpretation. For example, mothers are more likely to kill infants than older children because, according to Daly and Wilson, the mothers have invested much less in a very young child whereas older children are more likely to increase the mother's own inclusive fitness; this is significantly less marked as a trend in men because males do not have the relatively early limitation on reproductive ability that women do; and killing a mother who is closer to the end of her fertile years is correspondingly less costly to the inclusive fitness of the child than killing her when she is able to bear many children in the future.

Science, though, is a hard taskmaster. The figures that Daly and Wilson revealed do conform to a pattern that is explained by selfish gene theory but they are equally well accounted for by a cluster of alternative factors. There is no doubting that murder within families is mainly one of a spouse killing their partner rather than the murder-victim relationship being one of close genetic kinship, but this is not incontrovertible support for the existence of some kind of aggression inhibitor mechanism triggered by the sharing of genes. The spousal relationship is by definition a quite different one from that of, say, parent and child or grandchild. Spouses are usually much closer to one another in age and hence competing for resources in a way that genetic kin, except for sibs, do not. And by Daly and Wilson's own account – one which they make a lot of in a slightly different context – spousal sexual infidelity is a frequent cause of violence (their point precisely) and simply does not apply to close kin. Put differently, family relationships differ along a number of dimensions, and genetic kinship is just one of these. Age is another. Older mothers have a greater age difference from their children and hence are less likely to share interests and values with their children. This may seem an unlikely explanation for why when children do kill their parents they are usually elderly parents; but to many social scientists it is at least as plausible an argument as the claim that children are less inhibited in their violence to a close genetic relative when that relative has reduced capacity to increase the child's inclusive fitness. The same ambiguity of explanation applies to why it is younger mothers who kill their children rather than those who are older. Young mothers who kill their children are overwhelmingly people in straightened economic circumstances. They have less economic and, by definition, less psychological and social resources to fall back on for support. As to the different age distributions between men and women who kill their children, that too can be explained by differences in amount of child care that men and women undertake in western cultures at least.

Even the wicked stepparent explanation in terms of reduced genetic relationship between adult and child has been questioned, at least to an extent. A recent study of the murder of children in Sweden showed that when the killing of children aged 15 and under were examined, stepchildren were at no greater risk than were children living with their biological parents. However, Daly and Wilson reanalyzed that same data set correcting for the ages of the children (since their own data show younger children to be at greater risk than those who are older) and found that younger Swedish children were 10 times more likely to be killed by a stepparent than a biological parent. This supports their original contention, but it remains the case that the corrected data demonstrate a 10-fold difference between Sweden and north America, which suggests that cultural factors are intruding into these situations. Evolutionary psychologists will retort, correctly, than no one has ever doubted the intrusion of cultural factors into even the most hard-core of behaviors that are governed by human biology, like eating and sex; that other studies show parents spending significantly more on food, health and education of their own children than on their stepchildren; and they will also argue for the elegance of parsimonious explanation. Selfish gene theory provides a consistency of explanation, whereas the alternatives are a rather motley crew of age, parenting patterns, cultural practices, and the like. But in an animal as complex as humans where much of behavior is multiply determined and overdetermined, parsimony is a weak argument.

The response to this is to point to the range of behaviors that fall within the explanatory scope of evolutionary causation. In

1989 David Buss, also working out of a psychology department, published a study which had tested mate preferences in over 10,000 individuals drawn from 37 cultures located in six continents. The predictions came from sex selection theory and its elaboration by Trivers, the sociobiologist, in the early 1970s. Because the costs of gametes, gestation, and postnatal childcare fall disproportionately upon human females, their choice of mate should be weighted towards males who may provide "food, find or defend territories, defend the female against aggressors... feed and protect the young... provide opportunities for learning... transfer status, power or resources... and they may aid their offspring in forming reciprocal alliances." Males, however, "should prefer attributes in potential mates associated with reproductive value *or* fertility," the *or* referring to different views as to whether men sought short- or long-term mating partners during human evolutionary history. As in the case of Daly and Wilson, here was a study based directly in the sociobiology of 17 years before and focused on a highly specific feature of evolutionary theory. Here was no vague functionalist hand-waving of the Jamesian kind.

Because of the large scale of the study and its operation in countries of very different political climates and customs, people were questioned in ways appropriate to circumstances and the "samples obtained cannot be viewed as representative of the populations in each country." In spite of this, Buss claimed, the general finding was confirmation of the theoretical predictions: females, regardless of culture, choose mates who have cues indicating "resource acquisition" whereas males sought females who signaled "reproductive capacity." Buss' most consistent finding was that males prefer mates younger than themselves with females expressing reverse choices; in the majority of cultures women valued "good financial prospect" more in males than did the latter in females; "ambition and industriousness" were similarly more preferred by females than males; males in the majority of samples valued good looks more highly than females; the value assigned to chastity proved the least consistent finding of the study. Buss considered the data to be positive support for the predictions made, and a vindication of the evolutionary stance taken in the study of sex differences.

Once again the criticisms of the Buss study were many and varied. The anthropologist Mildred Dickemann, normally no enemy of biological explanations, was especially scathing. She considered Buss' methodology to be deeply flawed and his results to be at odds with consistent findings from in-depth anthropological studies which show wide cultural variations in sexual preferences and practices. Others pointed out that what people say and what they do are different. This is not a trivial matter and it points again to the multiple determination of human choices and actions. Yet others questioned differences in the cultures that Buss used, suggesting that much of the uniformity of his findings derived from cultural uniformity. One critic sardonically pointed to the cross-cultural practice of wearing business suits and how absurd it would be to postulate an innate and evolved cause for doing so.

Many of the difficulties that Buss and Daly and Wilson faced came from the use of observational studies. Data is collected from different agencies which have operated in different ways. The results are a surfeit of correlations, often complex statistical techniques, and an inability to manipulate variables systematically which would allow for conclusions about causes. That is why the work of Leda Cosmides, also published in 1989, was so important. It was a study of a very different kind from that of Buss and Daly and Wilson, but it too exemplified the move towards the application in psychology of specific aspects of evolutionary theory. Cosmides did not survey government figures or hand out questionnaires. Her's was an experimental approach and her chosen area was cognition. You don't get much more respectable academically in psychology than that. Here was an example of evolutionary thinking in psychology coming of age.

One of the most interesting developments in evolutionary psychology over the last decade and more has been the work of Gerd Gigerenzer and his colleagues at one of the Max Plank Institutes in Germany where the notion has been advanced of evolved heuristics as adaptive tools for reasoning, judging, and inferring, "in a fast and frugal way" across a range of problems from risk assessment to making decisions in choosing a mate. There is, in fact, a tradition on heuristics of thought that goes back to the beginnings of the cognitive revolution. In the 1960s an English psychologist, Peter Wason, had introduced a method for studying thinking in humans to see whether we reasoned in the manner approved by Popper for scientists. Wason created a reasoning task in which someone was presented with four cards, each bearing a letter on one side and a number on the other. Each was told a general rule and asked which cards must be turned over in order to determine the truth of the rule. The cards presented displayed a vowel, a consonant, an even number, and an odd number. The rule they were told to test was that if a card had a vowel on one side then it had an even number on the other side. Now the correct solution is to check the card showing the vowel *and* that with the odd number (to check whether the rule is disconfirmed). The card with the consonant can be ignored as can that showing the even number because the rule does not state what an even numbered card must have on its reverse side. In the language of logic, the cards, for example E, D, 8, and 7, correspond to P, not-P, Q, and not-Q. The correct solution is P (in the specific example, this is the card showing an E) and not-Q (the card displaying a 7). Almost everyone chose P and correctly ignored not-P, but many wrongly chose Q and equally incorrectly ignored not-Q. In Wason's words "the task proved to be peculiarly difficult," and was so even for people with formal training in logic. Only about one in ten people got it right. Most people seem biased to confirm a rule rather than disconfirm it.

However, it was then found that if the bloodless Ps and Qs are given familiar propositional content then most solve the problem with little difficulty. The famous example was the enforcement of age-related drinking laws: alcohol can only be drunk in a bar if the drinker is over 20 years of age. The cards then become drinking beer (P), drinking coke (not-P), being more than twenty years old (Q) and being under 20 (not-Q). Almost everyone understands that the ID of those drinking beer must be checked, as must the content of the glasses of those under 20. The age of someone drinking coke is irrelevant, as is what those over 20 are drinking. P and not-Q again. The explanation usually given for the ease with which the age-drink problem is solved is that age and drinking is a much practiced association in American culture, where this particular version of the Wason task was carried out, and that this experience facilitated the operation of an availability heuristic which is a general process that operates on any familiar input.

What Cosmides did was a clever variation on the Wason problem using unfamiliar propositional content. Her starting premise was that the evolution of the human mind during the two million or so years since the first species of the genus *Homo* appeared on the planet "would have produced special-purpose, domain-specific, mental algorithms – including rules of inference – for solving important and recurrent adaptive problems." In broad terms, this is a position very similar to Gigerenzer's heuristics of thought. One of the things we can be reasonably certain of is that human evolution occurred against the constant backdrop of selection for living in small social groups. From this she reasoned that in order to operate effectively as a group, and one in which some division of labor might be expected, rules of social exchange must operate such that the receiving of a benefit must be paid for by a cost, an action that fulfills some requirement that is to the gain of the group as a whole. Thus a domain of reasoning about social exchange, "social contract theory," would have evolved which must include a sensitivity to actions that cheat on the rules of social exchange. In order to test for the presence of a cheater-detector mechanism, she used a propositional language in the Wason task which, unlike the age-drinking situation, tested for circumstances which may have been typical when humans were evolving prior to the agricultural revolution. Since the propositional content centered on situations of foraging and food sharing never experienced before by her subjects, correct solutions could not be ascribed to the operation of an availability heuristic. In short, she predicted equal facility when solving unfamiliar problems as had occurred when the material was well known and much experienced. Her data confirmed her prediction and she claimed that what she had was evidence for a domain-specific form of reasoning that was essential to surviving, if not thriving, within a small, foraging social group. She also presented a reversal of the usual benefit-cost order of the proposition (if you want a benefit you must pay the cost), a switched social contract (if you have paid the cost you can have the benefit) in which, while the logically correct falsifiers remain the same, semantically the falsifiers become not-P and Q. Her findings were that in the switched contract her subjects did indeed identify the not-P and Q as potential cheaters to be scrutinized, thus confirming her general findings.

As always, critics begged to differ in their interpretations of Cosmides' interpretations. Many have argued that her data go no further than Wason's original finding that people are indeed biased in their thinking, but the bias is a more general one of being inclined to reason by confirmation rather than seeking instances that disconfirm reasoned conclusions. Indeed Popper's point was always that science is unique in its absolute reliance on discomformation – that is what makes science different from normal thinking. Others argued that her switched social contract predictably diverged from the original version of the problem because the structure of the logic was changed by the switch requiring alterations in the timing of actions. All of these criticisms are couched within the arcane and considerable technicalities of logic. What Cosmides had in her favor was a consistent commitment to a particular theoretical stance which she shared with the other evolutionary psychologists considered above.

The broad approach of these studies on extreme violence, mate choice, and social contract theory and cognition, along with others, were brought together in an influential volume of 1992 edited by Barkow, Cosmides, and Tooby entitled *The Adapted Mind*. What was referred to as the standard social science model, based on the generalizations of Boasian anthropology that culture can only be understood within its own terms and that humans are infinitely malleable because we come into this world as blank slates, was utterly rejected. Offered in its place was an "integrated causal model." It emphatically renounced any approach based on genetic differences between groups, insisted on the universality of an evolved structure of the human mind and outlined a program for an evolutionary psychology seeking to map out that structure and identify its principle psychological mechanisms. Broadly speaking three fundamental tenets were offered. The first is that the brain is a cluster of computers, each designed to generate behavior appropriate to specific environmental domains. The second is that the neural circuitry of each computing sector of the brain was designed by natural selection to solve problems in the environment of our ancestors. Third, different psychological mechanisms are the result of different complexes of neural networks specialized in solving different problems of adaptation. Thus, the mind is a set of adaptations, the explanation for which "lies completely in the past, starting one generation ago, and extending back across phylogenetic time to include the history of selection that constructed those designs" (this being a quotation from an earlier journal paper by Tooby and Cosmides).

The net result is what is sometimes described as the "Swiss-army knife" model of our stone-age minds, because what our minds are now is a product of the principle evolutionary forces acting on hominids during the Pleistocene (the period of time beginning about two million years ago to around 10 to 12 thousand years before the present). Little evolution of the mind could have occurred in the evolutionarily short space of time of just 12 millennia. Our minds now are no different from what they were 20,000 or perhaps even 30,000 years ago.

No psychological phenomena are considered to fall outside of this general explanatory model. In addition to emotional expression and recognition, the acquisition of language, the extraordinary capacity we have for remembering faces and for understanding number, less explored areas of academic psychology, like happiness, guilt, love, aggression, promiscuity, and rape, amongst many other psychological traits or behaviors, have all been considered within this general framework. Of these, two lines of additional study are worth considering briefly. The first is of historical importance, if nothing else, because Darwin himself had offered it as a process of importance in evolution. This is sexual selection: "the advantage which certain individuals have over others of the same sex and species solely in respect of reproduction" as he put it in *Descent* (which bore the subtitle *Selection in Relation to Sex*). Darwin used individual choice of mate, usually by the female, to explain a host of secondary sexual characteristics in males, like the coloration of fish, the tails of birds (famously, that of the peacock), and the antlers of deer. Wallace, however, was hostile to the notion, and the general attention of biology became fixated on natural selection. Geoffrey Miller argues that this form of selective scientific attention was a result of Victorian values and prudery in which sexual matters were not to be discussed, and certainly not the idea that females, human females, indulge in sexual choice. The great Ronald Fisher, cofounder of the modern synthesis (see chapter 4), did take sexual selection seriously, modeling how runaway selection might occur, but again the idea was either ignored or actively criticized and it was only in the 1980s that serious attention began to be paid to a selection force that operated in addition to that of natural selection: as a general theoretical structure in which natural selection gives rise to an additional level of selection, sexual selection is closely akin to evolutionary epistemology (chapter 5). In the present, sexual selection is widely recognized as an evolutionary force and considerable empirical data from animals support the reality of it. For example, reports in one of the April 2003 issues of *Science* shows how experimental manipulation of diet in male zebra finches and blackbirds, which results in enhanced immune system function and brighter bill color, also leads to increased female choice of males with more highly colored beaks.

As always, the question asked by evolutionary psychologists is whether what explains certain aspects of the evolution of other species should not also be seen to operate in humans. Could sexual selection have been a force in human evolution, and might it not still be a cause of some human behaviors? The answer must surely be yes on the grounds that humans are a species of animal and hence subject to the same biological laws as all other animals, but just how much it explains is debatable. One of the extraordinary features of hominid evolution has been the increase in brain size over the last two million years. The Australopithecine apes that immediately preceded the first species of *Homo* had a brain size similar to that of modern chimpanzees, which is about two and a half times larger than would be expected from body size. During hominid evolution that has spectacularly increased to around seven times that expected from body size. This is the most rapid increase in brain size within a lineage that is known, and may well be the most rapid that has ever occurred. What caused it? The general consensus is that brain size, after a correction has been made for the way in which brain size scales allometrically with body size, must, in an as yet unknown way, reflect intelligence. So this is a general line of argument that hominid intelligence has steadily increased. But why did it increase? Was modern human intelligence essential to survival in the Pleistocene? Did we really need to be able to invent culture, myths, and customs, do mathematics and write poetry to survive as foragers on the African savannah? The answer given by most commentators is no. Even evolutionary psychologists like Pinker have argued that skills like musicianship and storytelling, the ability both to do such things and also to appreciate them, are nonadaptive by-products of the natural selection of other, essential, features of the human mind. But others, like Miller, argue that sexual selection has been a rampant force in the evolution of the mind. "Sexual selection is the professional at sifting between genes. By comparison, natural selection is a rank amateur." Well, perhaps. Miller's is a powerful advocacy and the supporting arguments are strong. But we await evidence that, for example, artistic skill is linked to "good genes" and that musicianship in humans serves the same purpose, and even acts to affect female choice, as do those beaks in finches and blackbirds. It is also the case that many of Miller's claims, for example that the human head and the brain it encases, are rich in fitness information and hence strongly affect sexual selection, are just not supported with any data. One of the most prominent forms that fitness indicators take in the sexual selection literature is known as fluctuating asymmetry, which is a measure of the extent to which our bodily features which are paired (eyes, ears, limbs etc) vary from a precise bilateral symmetry. The assumption is that the more asymmetrical an individual is, the less good their genetic constitution is in resisting developmental stress brought about by, for example, infections. The more symmetrical someone is, the healthier they are and hence the better their genetic constitution. However, some biologists consider the relationship between fitness and fluctuating asymmetry to be highly tenuous. Moreover, there is no evidence that, for instance, female sexual preference has a genetic basis or that female choice and male facial symmetry covary with fitness, either now or in the past. This is an area of evolutionary psychology that is woefully short on evidence.

The other line of study is related to sexual selection in that instead of appealing to past selection pressures alone, it argues that the dynamics of the evolutionary process operating in the here and now provides the causal framework for understanding the psychological processes and mechanisms that can be observed, recorded and measured directly. It is also important because, like Cosmides' work, it takes evolutionary ideas into psychological territory that lies at the heart of the discipline. This is the family, and how the family forges human personality and character, a theme not only of a very important part of psychology, but also a recurrent theme of human storytelling that runs from Sophocles through the Old Testament and on to Shakespeare and beyond to the present. The work is owed to the American science historian Frank Sulloway and constitutes a continuous act of scholarship that extends close to three decades.

Sulloway's initial aim was to explain why people differ in their receptiveness to new ideas, and his principal vehicle in studying this has been individual responses to scientific innovation. But his ambition is wider than that: Sulloway wants to inject evolutionary explanation into all of history, and so his data come from biographical details of eminent people, usually scientists, the Protestant reformation, the French revolution and the voting patterns of United States Supreme Court judges, amongst other sources, all gathered to support the thesis that evolutionary forces are at work in the family, the consequence of which are personality types and personality differences.

Sulloway's general approach is to bring evolution into the family in two ways. One is the Trivers gene's-eye view of parent-offspring conflict and sibling rivalry as expounded by sociobiology. The other is to assert that Darwin's principle of divergence, the tendency for organisms to become adapted to diverse niches, applies to the family which offers children multiple niches within family space; this he combines with the principle of competitive exclusion, which holds that "no two species can coexist in the same habitat if their ecological requirements are identical". The essence of his approach is that it is the result of intra-family competition and the way this forces children to occupy particular family niches which then mold personality characters.

Children from the same family, Sulloway noted, are often as different from one another as they are from those of different families; and children occupying the same positions of birth order in different families are often very similar in personality. This he assumes is because the most important determiner of what niche within the family children will occupy is birth order. Firstborns from different families are much more similar to one another than they are to laterborns within the same family. Eldest children identify more closely with parents than do laterborns, and hence they identify more closely with authority in general. Firstborns are ambitious, conscientious, achievement-oriented, conventional, and defensive. They do well in environments that value such traits, and are much more likely to end up as Captains of Industry and as Presidents of professional associations than are laterborns. "Older siblings tend to preempt the most readily available niches, such as those associated with scholastic achievement and adult-like responsibility. As a consequence, younger siblings are impelled to make more unconventional choices that lead them down ever more radical pathways." In contrast to their more assertive and status-conscious sibs, laterborns are more easy-going, flexible, questioning, less certain of themselves, and more open to new ideas.

One school of personality theory assumes the existence of a small set of basic personality traits which we all have to a greater or lesser degree. The traits exist in all of us, but where we lie along the dimension of each trait is determined in part by experience. Sulloway adopted the "big five" version of this theory and proceeded to examine his data on the basis of how birth order affects each trait (extraversion, neuroticism, agreeableness, conscientiousness, and openness to experience). A meta-analysis of 196 studies involving over 120,000 subjects showed hugely significant effects for openness to experience and agreeableness, which predominate amongst laterborns; firstborns are significantly more conscientious. Extraversion and neuroticism are not determined by birth order.

Leaving aside modern data, he then combed through the historical record of about 6,000 lives lived over the last six centuries, including some 3,900 scientists. Amongst his main concerns was to ascertain the openness to experience of these people as evidenced by those who embraced new ideas and those who rejected them. Some of his findings are stunning. Across all major scientific revolutions of the last 500 years Sulloway showed that laterborns were some six to seven times more likely to support new ideas than were firstborns. Strikingly, when, as with eugenics and vitalism, the scientific theories have been conservative in the sense that conceptually they are consonant with the prevailing social and political views of the ruling classes, then and only then did firstborn support for them exceed those of laterborns. Theories of evolution presented fine examples of revolutionary ideas finding overwhelming support amongst laterborns, but not first children.

This is evolutionary psychology with knobs on. Like previous examples, Sulloway's work is a paragon of the principle of specific application. Where it differs from other areas of evolutionary psychology is in its subject matter. Psychologists of the "whole person" variety, as opposed to those whose expertise lies in fundamental mechanisms like memory or perception, are unanimous in their view of the crucial psychological significance of the family, that relatively stable small social group within which the child is raised. Nothing is more important, they claim, than our families in making us the kinds of people we end up being for the rest of our lives. Fascinating, and important, as are murder rates within families, reproductive strategies and sexual choices, and innate cognitive algorithms, as *psychology*, perhaps, they pale into insignificance when put alongside family dynamics and its consequences. In bringing evolution into the family Sulloway has brought evolutionary ideas into psychology in an unprecedented manner. Once again criticism is possible – it almost always is. Some of the most original and significant scientists of all time, like Newton, Kepler, Galileo, and Einstein, were firstborns. Most of his subjects lived in rather different times to now when sibships were three or four times the size they are in modern times. We need studies on modern families with their much smaller numbers of children. And we certainly need cross-cultural studies. We need to know, for example, whether the personality differences arising from birth order that Sulloway reports are present also in hunter-gatherer cultures.

The studies described here, whilst among the most prominent, are merely representative of a general viewpoint that has grown to significant proportions. Evolutionary psychology rules no area of a science of mind out of understanding within an evolutionary framework. In effect it has appropriated all of modern psychological science and added to it an evolutionary perspective. This is not a negative judgment, merely a reflection of the ambition of the discipline. The specific criticisms attaching to each of the studies outlined above are a part of the normal hurly-burly of science. There are, however, more general criticisms that have been leveled at attempts to understand psychology from an evolutionary perspective, criticisms which often seem to be driven by nonscientific considerations, and it is to these that we briefly turn.

Which Side is Bringing Science into Disrepute?

It would be incorrect to judge the furor over the application of sociobiology to humans as a mere curtain-raiser to what was to come with the appearance of evolutionary psychology in the 1980s. But what is clear is that the principal (in the sense of most visible, and most visible because they are or were significant contributors to their own areas of science) critics of the earlier era maintained their same stances with regard to evolutionary psychology on their more substantive points. The trivial nonsense and unpleasant *ad hominem* attacks, from both sides, can be sampled in mid-1990s copies of the *New York Review of Books*, though these tasteless displays of professional spite are best forgotten. In general the criticisms came as two types, the substantive and the fatuous.

The fatuous, often motivated by considerations other than science, come broadly in three forms. One is the view that all evolutionary psychologists are as one and that evolutionary psychology is one thing. In one sense this is trivially true. But in another, it is incorrect. All evolutionary psychologists seek *an* evolutionary explanation of some kind for the phenomena that they study. But within that broad framework the kinds of explanation are as diverse as adaptationist accounts on the one hand and those of evolutionary epistemology on the other. It is also the case that the methodologies used encompass a broad range with manifest differences between, say, on the one hand someone pursuing an analysis of decision making through a game theoretic analysis, and on another, differences in reproductive strategies in men and women, and on a third hand, a memetic analysis of changes in the way people within a specific industry understand market responses to their product. Such obvious differences are invisible only to the ignorant or the vindictive. In a very real sense there are many different ways of doing, and thinking about, evolutionary psychology. Apart from rejecting the application of evolutionary theory as a whole to all of psychology – in other words, a blanket assertion that evolution cannot or should not be applied to any understanding of the human mind – there is no single criticism that applies to all of the subject.

The second is the assumption that at least some evolutionary psychologists have an ideological axe to grind, and that it is of the extreme political right. There has to be a modicum of truth to this. There are some racist evolutionary psychologists out there; and an evolutionary psychologist gave evidence in the defense of a notorious holocaust-denier in a libel trial in London a few years ago. There may even be some who do commit the naturalistic fallacy (confusing is with ought). But there are also racist physicists (some quite notorious) and botanists who support political parties of the far right, and nobody is silly enough to think that this impugns their sciences. The accusation simply brings science into disrepute. But if some critics find it possible to imply that evolutionary psychology is a tool of right-wing ideology and a form of social Darwinism then, in part, it is because the lessons of the sociobiology wars were not properly learned. There undoubtedly have been instances of crass and crude analysis with a marked inability to understand that most of human behavior is multiply determined, together with an abject failure to anticipate the gifts of criticism been made to those who oppose natural science approaches to the human mind. If the criticism holds, it holds to specific individuals.

The third of the fatuous criticisms is that any approach that considers at least some aspects of the mind to be the product of evolution must, and does, imply genetic part causation and hence is an exercise in reductionist thinking. This is a *non sequitur*. Genetic part causation does not rule out causes based also in individual development, individual learning, or enculturation. Multiple determination of psychological traits is as widely accepted by psychologists seeking evolutionary explanations as it is by those who do not have that theoretical orientation. There is another and equally incorrect aspect of this form of criticism. This is the idea, put forward by some surprisingly senior psychologists, that assumptions of evolution and genetic part causation relieves one of the need to do any further science – that evolutionists just label mechanisms and traits as evolved and innate and believe the science complete. This is a criticism of such nonsensical proportions that it is hard to understand the motivation behind it.

Another feature of the accusation of genetic reductionism is that some evolutionary psychologists rely upon the Lorenzian insight of learning as an evolved trait. But how can adhering to the view of evolved cognitive modules be considered a reductionist stance? It manifestly is not. There is another way of saying this: when intelligence of any kind evolved, the causal understanding of intelligent behavior shifted partially from genes to neural networks. Thus no explanation of intelligent behavior can ever be considered reductionist. In general, accusations of reductionism are made by those with a nonscientific axe to grind.

There are four substantive criticisms, and none apply to every form of evolutionary psychology. The first is the notion of the environment of evolutionary adaptedness (EEA), an idea first put forward, as noted in chapter 6, by the psychoanalyst John

Bowlby, and adopted by many evolutionary psychologists reliant upon the notion of the mind as a bundle of adaptations. The core idea is that the Pleistocene, the geological period which saw the first appearance of members of the genus *Homo*, is that environment and it was to the conditions of this two million year period to which the human mind is adapted. This is an error on two counts, but even if accepted as correct, a weakness on another. The first error is that much of what is the human mind now existed prior to the appearance of *Homo habilis*. These would include traits as diverse as basic motivational states, associative learning, working memory, nonverbal communication and visual scene construction, to mention but a few. Some of these traits, such as conditioning, are likely scores, even hundreds, of millions of years old. We cannot be sure when these traits first evolved, but we do know with certainty from their phylogenetic distribution that they long predate the Pleistocene.

The second error is the assumption inherent in the phrase that the Pleistocene comprised a single environment. It obviously did not. Every reconstruction of the last two million years postulates enormous climate change, for example, and changes in climate would have led to chains of changes in other circumstances, like food resources. As said earlier, the only likely single circumstance that was invariant during human evolution was that life was lived in relatively small social groups. One defense of the EEA concept is that, as expressed by Tooby and Cosmides, it is a "statistical composite." But as the excellent Laland and Brown ask, "how could one compute a statistical composite of all the relevant environments encountered by our ancestors, and weight them accordingly?" The simple answer is you can't.

The weakness of the EEA concept is tied to the problems encountered by adaptationist accounts of the mind of every kind. The insistence that the adaptations are to past environments and hence that their explanation "lies completely in the past" makes them empirically inaccessible – which, in effect, takes them out of the realm of science and imprisons it within speculative narrative. Even the best of archaeological evidence can be interpreted in many ways with regard to necessary psychological mechanisms. For example, a not infrequent speculation concerns the sudden appearance of decorative artifacts, be they ostrich eggshell beads or wall paintings, which suddenly appear about 40,000 to 50,000 years ago. What happened to the human mind to allow the sudden (but was it sudden?) appearance of symbols? Some argue for the capacity to understand that each life ends in death, some for the evolution of language, others for imitation, and yet others for mimesis. The order in which these might have evolved also varies between speculative accounts. But there is no evidence to support when any one or other of these first appeared, much less their ordering in time. For example, Phillip Tobias argues for language in *H.habilis* two million years ago; others, on the basis of these symbolic artifacts, for its late appearance less than a hundred thousand years before the present, and there are any number of arguments for timing between these two extremes. The fact is we do not know with anything approaching scientific certainty any of these things. Explanations of adaptations based on past events are not a part of science.

One of the oddities of the assertion that the adaptations of the human mind can only be understood in terms of the human past is that so much of human behavior in the here and now, and their accompanying psychological mechanisms, has obvious adaptive value that we can indeed put our empirical hands on. Choosing mates, sharing resources, recognizing faces, acquiring communication skills including language, the attribution of intentional mental states, defending oneself, nurturing one's children, amongst many others, are often sited as adaptive traits that arose in the Pleistocene in response to the supposed constant selection pressures of that time. Well, perhaps, but so what? They are present now, can and are being investigated now, and it is called psychology. Declaring a present trait an adaptation to the past is an odd way to do science.

A lesser criticism of claims that psychological traits are adaptations is that actually they may be exaptations. It is obvious that writing and reading, which first appeared as Sumerian script about 3,200 B.C., is not an adaptation. It is an amalgam of linguistic, visual, and manual skills, each of which itself is an adaptation, but which brought together results in a trait that serves a different function. This, by the definition offered earlier in this chapter, makes writing and reading exaptations. But does this matter? Some think not. As the philosopher Daniel Dennett notes "no function is eternal" and every structure must have evolved out of some predecessor structure whose functions might have been different or nonexistent. In other words, all adaptations are exaptations. The problem, if it is one at all, is that some very important psychological traits, like language, are exaptations; and that most human of all characteristics, culture, is caused by several human-specific psychological mechanisms, including language. So the human mind might comprise exaptations which are themselves exaptations of exaptations. This does not detract from an adaptationist approach, but it does indicate a science of adaptations that is very much more complex than that with which biology has previously dealt.

A third major criticism is that evolutionary psychology is too preoccupied with domain specificity and the notion of a modular mind (the Swiss army knife analogy), and that to the extent that the mind is modular it pays insufficient attention to the possibility that it becomes so by general learning processes formed by way of developmental processes. There are two responses to this. The one is that development can be only partly responsible for constraining the structure of the mind and brain. Individual experience is too varied for such experience alone to cause the uniformity of psychological processes and mechanisms that every human being, pathology apart, possesses. If development is what is doing the constraining then something must be causing those developmental constraints. Since all development begins with the fertilized egg, and that egg contains the evolved genes that determine our species' identity, it is simply inconceivable that genes are not part responsible for the structure and function of our minds. The second response is that this is an empirical matter which theory alone will not resolve.

My task has been to list the criticisms, and neither to support nor refute them. Yet even if these criticisms are correct, they are correctable. All can be taken into account in the construction of a more powerful evolutionary psychology. The fourth major criticism, some social scientists argue, fatally flaws the whole enterprise. This is that human culture, which shapes our psychology itself and is a major determiner of what humans do and think, is a force wholly different from biological evolution and cannot be encompassed by any form of evolutionary theory. Shedding my impartiality on the other major criticisms, it must be said that this is quite simply incorrect, and it is to this that we now turn.

A Natural Science of Culture

In the 1860s Wallace, codiscoverer of natural selection, began to write of the importance of the accumulation of knowledge and skills in human evolution; he believed that once human intelligence had reached the level that sustained culture that the evolution of the human mind by natural selection ceased and all further human evolution occurred at the cultural level. In forwarding the notion of cultural change as cultural evolution, Wallace was about a century ahead of his time. Conway Lloyd Morgan was also a cultural evolutionist, as was James Mark Baldwin. But with biology outlawed from the study of culture by Boas and his disciples in anthropology, which was the principal science of culture throughout the twentieth century, these were voices without influence. Psychology itself was too sprawling a subject to lay great emphasis on culture. Certainly important individuals such as Freud made forays into culture but these were always secondary to issues such as multilevel conceptions of pathology; and the social psychologists who understood how crucial culture is to a science of mind simply did not command the central conceptual ground of psychology the way, say, the learning theorists did. This neglect suited the social scientists. Psychology really does occupy the scientific borderlands between the natural and social sciences. This is what makes it a uniquely important science, but to Boas' intellectual heirs, that was good reason to keep clear of psychology, even from the behaviorism whose environmentalism made it a natural bedfellow of cultural anthropology.

There is an asymmetry of regard, though, between psychologists for whom evolution is central and other psychologists as well as other social scientists at large. It is that, just as in the exceptional case of Baldwin, while culture is considered as an essential part of a science of mind to most evolutionists, those whose traditions lie in the study of culture and culture alone have little regard for the theory of evolution, and often times little regard for biology in any form. Thus while many cultural anthropologists assume that culture is a phenomenon *sui generis*, in contrast the 1992 volume which has come to assume seminal importance amongst evolutionary psychologists had the subtitle *Evolutionary Psychology and the Generation of Culture*; the first chapter was *The Psychological Foundations of Culture* by Tooby and Cosmides.

There are three general approaches to establishing links between culture and evolution. The least relevant to psychology is gene-culture coevolutionary theory. The general conception is of two parallel and interconnected tracks of evolutionary change in time, one biological and the other cultural, with some necessary degree of causal linkage between the two. The classic case study by Cavalli-Sforza and Feldman in the 1970s is the linkage between the biological evolution of lactose tolerance amongst certain social groups in northern Europe and the cultural evolution that resulted in animal husbandry and dietary practices as farming spread from the middle east into these north westerly regions. Notable later contributors included Boyd and Richerson. The modeling is important, but as with population genetics which could be developed without having to know the details of the underlying genetics, the means of transmission and the psychological processes and mechanisms of the cultural track of evolution are something of an irrelevance to that modeling.

A not unsimilar bias is present in memetics, which has been a second way of trying to establish links between biology and culture. As seen in chapter 5, Baldwin advanced what is now clearly recognizable as memetics. In 1956 the anthropologist George Murdock toyed with the idea that culture and cultural change might be understood as a system analogous to the transformation of species by evolution. At about the same time, and fulfilling the same conceptual program of Baldwin 60 years before, Donald Campbell began to proselytize universal Darwinism, which necessarily included the conception of cultural change as evolutionary in form. In 1976 Richard Dawkins devoted the final chapter of' *The Selfish Gene* to "Memes: the new replicators." Dawkins offered the meme as a cultural analogue of the gene and the very final sentence of this classic book describes memes as the means by which humans escape "the tyranny of the selfish replicators." But whether memetics can be transformed into a viable science is debatable (some of that debate can be found in Aunger's collection of essays). It certainly will not constitute a satisfactory account of human culture as long as it pursues the mistaken view that all memes are unitary in nature and transmitted by imitation. It is, to social scientists, an egregious error to conflate something like skirt length with patriotism, even though both are instances of culture; and it is an equally grave error, psychologically, to think that we learn the difference between a restaurant and a prison in the same way that we acquire a motor skill like using a knife and fork even though both are transmitted between cultural generations.

The third approach is to take the view that, whatever forms of culture other species have (and it is clear that other species of ape as well as a number of species of cetacea – whales and dolphins – do have culture), human culture is unique to us and arises from species-specific psychological mechanisms that define our species psychologically. This is eminently do-able science but it needs to guard itself against the persistent criticism that cultural scientists have leveled at biological approaches to their subject for many decades, which is death by over-simplification. A great deal of what humans think and do is caused by the cultures in which they live. This includes our deaths often enough – a survey of warfare in the twentieth century shows it to be caused over-whelmingly by social constructions like ideologies, religions, ethnicity, and spheres of political and economic influence. The ethological and primitive sociobiological notions that warfare is caused by aggressive instincts or increases in inclusive fitness by the victors gaining access to women are hopelessly incomplete accounts, with the possible exception of some limited social groups like the Yanomamo peoples of South America. Such simple-minded and crass explanations of warfare really do bring evolutionary psychology into disrepute. One has only to consider the recent wars in Iraq and Afghanistan to understand why social scientists and historians view such ideas with contempt.

Social constructions are entities like money and justice that exist only because the members of a culture agree that they exist. They are complex and powerful determiners of human behavior. They are bound into our neural networks, and particu-larly the way the neural networks of one human interacts and interleaves with those of another. They do not lie outside of our biology, however. They are explicable as products of human history, both evolutionary and individual. Whether modern human culture evolved in the way that our circulatory systems evolved is unclear. Certainly culture is an exaptation, because some of its principal psychological mechanisms, like language and theory of mind, are themselves exaptations. So the complexity of culture is going to stretch evolutionary theory further than has ever been the case before. But no serious scholar has ever thought that a science of the human mind is going to be easy, particularly a science of mind that will conceptually marry evolutionary theory and human cultural complexity.

CHAPTER EIGHT

Future Prospects

It is clear from the previous chapters that until recently evolution has had only a minor presence within psychology. This remains the case, there being a curious disjunction between the considerable interest shared by many in human origins, especially the origins of our minds, and the small place the theory of evolution has within academic psychology. Accessible accounts relating any aspect of psychology to evolution receive attention in the mass media on a scale that works on geology or crystallography can never aspire to. Gifted writers like Steven Pinker and Geoffrey Miller are always reviewed in professional journals like *Science* and *Nature,* as well as appearing in the book sections of popular newspapers. Yet within psychology itself this kind of visibility is simply absent. By any measure one cares to use – numbers of pages in general texts, courses taught in university departments of psychology, numbers of academic staff, research grants, journals – evolution has but a minor role to play in the discipline as it exists now.

It is no business of history to consider the future, but even that arch critic of evolutionary psychology, the late Stephen J. Gould, wrote thus in 1991:

> It would be the most extraordinary happening in all intellectual history if the cardinal theory for understanding the biological origin and construction of our brains and bodies had no insights to offer to disciplines that study the social organizations arising from such evolved mental power. (Gould, 1991, p. 51)

In this he was surely correct. So while the small hold that evolutionary thought now has in psychology is secure, there are reasons to believe that it will grow and expand, especially when these reasons inevitably are joined one to another. These can be quickly laid out.

The first lies in the growing realization amongst psychologists of the truth of Gould's assertion. The central theorem of biology simply must have a place within a science of mind. It is obviously the case that psychology can grow and thrive without paying any regard to evolution. Like liver function or the structure of the endocrine system, memory or cognitive development can, and most usually have, been studied in terms of proximate causes without any need for recourse to evolutionary explanation. However, if it is a complete science of any psychological process or mechanism that is sought, one that encompasses all causes, then evolution cannot be left out of the account any more than it can be omitted from a complete explanation of any other biological phenomenon.

The second reason for optimism lies in the inevitable improvements in understanding just how the human mind is structured, as well as that of our closest living relatives. Knowledge of cognition in nonhuman apes, of just how these particular joints of nature are to be carved and how they fit together, has increased in leaps and bounds in recent years. So too has understanding of human cognition. It is only in the last couple of decades, for example, that we have come to see the importance of the attribution of intentional mental states (theory of mind) to others in the cognitive development of the child. The stages by which this occurs, and the catastrophic consequences of the failure of this capacity, is relatively recently gained knowledge. The result of such improved understanding in both humans and nonhuman primates will be an appreciation of what is truly unique to our minds and just how exactly we differ from chimpanzees and other great apes.

Such advances will be paralleled by those occurring in the neurosciences and genetics. This is the third reason for optimism. New technologies and clever experiments are leading to greater understanding, particularly of how to carve the brain at the joints that map onto psychological structure and function. Add to that the inevitable advances that will be made in the human genome project, especially in the light of the announcement made in September of 2003 of the launch of a massive extension to that project on how genes shape brain development and function, and just how genes transform into the myriad of proteins that form the building blocks of cells, including nerve cells, and the resultant neurogenetics will allow a triple alliance of genetics, brain structure, and psychological function to form a true multidisciplinary science of mind.

The importance of this to an evolutionary understanding of the mind becomes clear when to this cocktail of future science is added two extraordinary studies published in 1997 and 2000 on Neanderthal DNA, and one from 2003 on that of relatively ancient *Homo sapiens*. The first of these in the journal *Cell* detailed the findings from the sequencing of mitochondrial DNA extracted from the bones of the very first specimen of Neanderthal found in the Neander valley and described in the 1850s. Mitochondria are tiny subcellular organelles that are the powerhouses of the cell, extracting from food the energy that drives all the cells' processes and activities. The mitochondria contain DNA in small circular chromosomes which is inherited from the cytoplasm of the mother since human sperm, and that of most species, contain no mitochondria. Because there are many mitochondria in almost all cell types, mitochondrial DNA is easier to access in fossil tissue than that which is present in the chromosomes of the nucleus, the nuclear DNA which is inherited from both mother and father. What the 1997 report showed was that contrary to one theory of modern human origins, *Homo sapiens* and *Homo neanderthalensis* diverged from a common ancestry between about 550,000 and 690,000 years ago. In other words, Neanderthals were not ancestral to modern humans, both species sharing a common *Homo erectus* origin, one probably very similar to *Homo heidelbergensis*. The 2000 paper in *Nature* confirmed this finding with exquisite detail using a Neanderthal specimen from the Balkans, some 2,500 km from the Neander valley, and dated with reasonable accuracy to have lived about 29,000 years before the present. Then in May 2003 Caramelli and others confirmed these findings in a paper in the *Proceedings of the National Academy of Sciences* which compared mitochondrial DNA extracted from anatomically modern *Homo sapiens* specimens dated to around 23 to 25 thousand years before the present with those of present-day humans and Neanderthals. The results showed that the mitochondrial DNA of humans that lived more than 20 millennia ago "fall well within the range of variation of today's humans," but are markedly different from those available sequences from Neanderthals.

It is nuclear DNA, not that of the mitochondria, that determines phenotypic characters like the structure of the brain, and so far it has not proved possible to sequence ancient nuclear DNA. But this is likely to change as molecular biology technology advances, as it surely will. It is very probable that nuclear DNA from *Homo sapiens* dating from between 20,000 and 10,000 years before the present will be sequenced. That of chimpanzees is being sequenced as this is written.

That Neanderthals were not ancestral to modern humans is an important finding, but the real point is that we are looking to a future when genomic and proteomic knowledge of modern humans, ancient humans, and modern nonhuman apes will be allied to understanding of the genetic and neurological bases of psychological mechanisms. Such cross-species comparisons and their implications will demand evolutionary interpretation. Then evolutionary explanation will no longer be a mere option for psychologists with an interest in biological theory. It will become an absolute requirement for completing understanding of how we humans of today have minds that enable us to understand the origins of those minds.

References

PREFACE

Richards, Robert J. (1987) *Darwin and the Emergence of Evolutionary Theories of Mind and Behavior*. Chicago, Chicago University Press.

CHAPTER 2

Ayer, A. (1980) *Hume*. Oxford, Oxford University Press.

Barnes, J. (1982) Aristotle. In R.M. Hare, Jonathan Barnes, and Henry Chadwick, *Founders of Thought*. Oxford, Oxford University Press.

Dunn, S. (1984) *Locke*. Oxford, Oxford University Press.

Hare, R.M. (1982) Plato. In R.M. Hare, Jonathan Barnes, and Henry Chadwick, *Founders of Thought*. Oxford, Oxford University Press.

Mayr, Ernst (1982) *The Growth of Biological Thought*. Cambridge, MA, Harvard University Press.

Nidditch, P. (ed.) (1975) *Locke: Essay Concerning Human Understanding*. Oxford, Clarendon Press.

Richards, Robert J. (1987) *Darwin and the Emergence of Evolutionary Theories of Mind and Behavior*. Chicago, Chicago University Press.

CHAPTER 3

Boakes, R. (1984) *From Darwin to Behaviourism*. Cambridge, Cambridge University Press.

Boring, E.G. (1953, 2nd edn) *A History of Experimental Psychology*. New York, Appleton-Century-Croft.

Darwin, C. (1871) *The Descent of Man and Selection in Relation to Sex*. London, Murray.

Darwin, C. (1872/1958 6th edn) *The Origin of Species*. New York, Mentor Books.

Knight, M. (1950) *William James*. London, Penguin Books.

Leahey, T.H. (1987) *A History of Psychology*. Englewood Cliffs, Prentice-Hall.

Sulloway, F.J. (1979) *Freud, Biologist of the Mind*. London, André Deutsch.

CHAPTER 4

Barrs, B.J. (1986) *The Cognitive Revolution in Psychology*. New York, Guilford Press.

Bronowski, J. (1973) *The Ascent of Man*. London, BBC publications.

Darwin, C. (1871) *The Descent of Man and Selection in Relation to Sex*. Toronto, Random House Modern Library.

Degler, C.N. (1991) *In Search of Human Nature: The Decline and Revival of Darwinism in American Social Thought*. Oxford, Oxford University Press.

Freeman, D. (1983) *Margaret Mead and Samoa: The Making and Unmaking of an Anthropological Myth*. Cambridge, MA, Harvard University Press.

Ridley, M. (1996 2nd edn) *Evolution*. Oxford, Blackwell Publishers.

Watson, J.B. (1913) Psychology as the behaviorist views it. *Psychological Review*, vol. 20, 158–77.

Watson, J.B. (1924) *Behaviorism*. Chicago, University of Chicago Press.

CHAPTER 5

Baldwin, J.M. (1909) *Darwin and the Humanities*. Baltimore, Review Publishing.

Broughton, J.M. and Freeman-Moir, J.M. (1982) *The Cognitive-Developmental Psychology of James Mark Baldwin*. Northwood, NJ, Ablex Publishing.

Campbell, D.T. (1974) Evolutionary Epistemology. In P.A. Schilpp (ed.) *The Philosophy of Karl Popper*, Book 1, pp. 413–63. La Salle, IL, Open Court Publishing.

Edelman, G. (1987) *Neural Darwinism*. New York, Basic Books.

Huxley, T.H. (1869) *Critiques and Addresses*. London, Macmillan.

James, W. (1880) Great men, great thoughts, and the environment. *The Atlantic Monthly*, vol. XLVI, 441–59.

Oppenheim, R.W. (1982) Preformation and epigenesis in the origins of the nervous system and behaviour: Issues, concepts and their history. In P.P.G. Bateson and P.H. Klopfer (eds) *Perspectives in Ethology, vol. 5 Ontogeny*, pp. 1–100. New York, Plenum.

Plotkin, H. (1994) *The Nature of Knowledge*. London, Allen Lane.

Richards, R.J. (1987) James Mark Baldwin: Evolutionary Biopsychology and the Politics of Scientific Ideas. In *Darwin and the Emergence of*

Evolutionary Theories of Mind and Behaviour. Chicago, Chicago University Press.

Waddington, C.H. (1975) *The Evolution of an Evolutionist.* Edinburgh, Edinburgh University Press.

CHAPTER 6

Chagnon, N.A. and Irons, W. (1979) *Evolutionary Biology and Human Social Behavior: An Anthropological Perspective.* North Scituate, MA, Duxberry Press.

Dawkins, R. (1976) *The Selfish Gene.* Oxford, Oxford University Press.

Eisenberg, L. (1973) The human nature of human nature. *Science,* vol. 176, 123–8.

Krebs, J.R. and Davies, N.B. (1993 3rd edn) *An Introduction to Behavioural Ecology.* Oxford, Blackwell Publishers.

Nisbett, A. (1976) *Konrad Lorenz.* London, Dent and Son.

Nobel Prize website: Konrad Lorenz autobiography – http://www.nobel.se/medicine/laureates/1973/lorenz-autobio.

Schiller, C.H. (1957) *Instinctive Behaviour: The Development of a Modern Concept.* London, Methuen.

Segerstrale, U. (2000) *Defenders of the Truth: The Sociobiology Debate.* Oxford, Oxford University Press.

Thorpe, W.H. (1979) *The Origins and Rise of Ethology.* London, Heinemann.

Tinbergen, N. (1951) *The Study of Instinct.* Oxford, Clarendon Press.

Wilson, E.O. (1975) *Sociobiology: The New Synthesis.* Cambridge, MA, Harvard University Press.

CHAPTER 7

Aunger, R. (ed.) (2000) *Darwinizing Culture: The Status of Memetics as a Science.* Oxford, Oxford University Press.

Barkow, J.W., Cosmides, L., and Tooby, J. (eds) (1992) *The Adapted Mind: Evolutionary Psychology and the Generation of Culture.* Oxford, Oxford University Press.

Buss, D.M. (1989) Sex differences in human mate preferences: Evolutionary hypotheses tested in 37 cultures. *Behavioural and Brain Sciences,* vol. 12, 1–49.

Cosmides, L. and Tooby, J. (1990) The past explains the present: Emotional adaptations and the structure of ancestral environments. *Ethology and Sociobiology,* vol. 11, 375–424.

Daly, M. and Wilson, M. (1988a) *Homicide.* New York, Aldine.

Daly, M. and Wilson, M. (1988b) Evolutionary psychology and family homicide. *Science*, vol. 242, 519–24.

Gigerenzer, G (2000) *Adaptive Thinking: Rationality in the Real World*. Oxford, Oxford University Press.

Hauser, M.D., Chomsky, N., and Fitch, W.T. (2002) The faculty of language: What is it, who has it, and how did it evolve? *Science*, vol. 298, 1569–79.

Laland, K.N. and Brown, G.R. (2002) *Sense and Nonsense: Evolutionary Perspectives on Human Behaviour*. Oxford, Oxford University Press.

Mandler, G. (1996) The situation of psychology: Landmarks and choice points. *American Journal of Psychology*, vol. 109, 1–35.

Marler, P. and Terrace, H.S. (1984) *The Biology of Learning (Dahlem workshops proceedings)*.

Miller, G. (2000) *The Mating Mind*. London, Heinemann.

Odling-Smee, F.J., Laland, K.N., and Feldman, M.W. (2003) *Niche Construction: The Neglected Process in Evolution*. Princeton, NJ, Princeton University Press.

Pinker, S. (2002) *The Blank Slate*. London, Allen Lane.

Plotkin, H. (2002) *The Imagined World Made Real: Towards a Natural Science of Culture*. London, Allen Lane.

Sulloway, F.J. (1996) *Born to Rebel*. New York, Pantheon Books.

CHAPTER 8

Caramelli, D., Lalueza-Fox, C., Vernesi, C., Lari, M., Casoli, A., Mallegni, F., Chiarelli, B., Dupanloup, Bertranpetit, J., Barbujani, G., and Bertorelle, G. (2003) Evidence for a genetic discontinuity between Neandertals and 24,000-year-old anatomically modern Europeans. *Proceedings of the National Academy of Sciences*, vol. 100, 6593–7.

Gould, S.J. (1991) Exaptation: A crucial tool for an evolutionary psychology. *Journal of Social Issues*, vol. 47, 43–65.

Krings, M., Stone, A., Schmitz, R.W., Krainitzki, H., Stoneking, M., and Paabo, S. (1997) Neanderthal DNA sequences and the origin of modern humans. *Cell*, vol. 90, 19–30.

Ovchinnikov, I.V., Gotherstrom, A., Romanova, G.P., Kharitinov, V.M., Liden, K., and Goodwin, W. (2000) Molecular analysis of Neanderthal DNA from the northern Caucasus. *Nature*, vol. 404, 490–3.

Index